Naturalist's Guide to Observing Nature

Kurt Rinehart

STACKPOLE
BOOKS

Published by
STACKPOLE BOOKS
5067 Ritter Road
Mechanicsburg, PA 17055
www.stackpolebooks.com

Printed in the United States of America

10 9 8 7 6 5 4 3 2 1

First Edition

Library of Congress Cataloging-in-Publication Data

Rinehart, Kurt.
  Naturalist's guide to observing nature / Kurt Rinehart.—1st ed.
     p. cm.
   ISBN-13: 978-0-8117-3268-0
  1. Natural history. 2. Nature. I. Title.

QH45.2.R56 2006
508—dc22

                                                        2005037380

Naturalist's Guide
to Observing Nature

To Cole and Hazel

Contents

Acknowledgments

My deepest thanks go to my wonderful wife, Susie. She not only put up with my late nights in the office but also helped organize and edit the book while working full time and taking care of our children, leaving precious little time for her own book projects. Mark Elbroch was, and remains, a generous and enthusiastic supporter and friend. Without his encouragement, I never would have believed that I could write a book, nor known how to go about doing so. I'm grateful to Jon Young who brought natural history to life in a personal, narrative way and helped me to know one place intimately. I owe tremendous thanks to everyone at the Mountain School these past few years, Jack Childs and Emil McCain of the Borderlands Jaguar Project, and David Hirth at the Rubenstein School for the Environment and Natural Resources (University of Vermont) for their praise and patience. My family's support of my naturalist tendencies and my dad's intense curiosity of the natural world planted the seed of this book long ago.

Introduction

This book is devoted to enhancing your ability to identify what you see by tapping into your own observations of bird, mammal, and plant location and behavior. It will teach you how to unravel an ambiguous sighting by drawing on field observations as well as field guides and other resources. The goal is to develop something like a dialogue between field and field guide. Your job is to ask the right questions, adopt the right perspectives in the field, and draw all the information you can out of your guides. The perspective you learn here will not only guide your observations but also help you pick up lots of great information.

Most of us start with one simple question when observing nature: What is it? Turning to a field guide, the question becomes, What does it look like? But when someone asks for my help in identifying some bird or track, my first question is, Where was it?

Last year a friend who lives nearby on a hilltop farm started learning about the birds in the area. She would tell me each new bird she identified, and one morning she told me that she had seen a junco. I asked a few questions about the sighting, beginning with where she had seen it. Her response—up on the hill near the big garden—seemed a little funny to me. I wouldn't expect to see juncos out on that open hill, with its acres of garden and surrounding pastures. It was possible, but I had to probe deeper. Next, I asked one question to refine my sense of the bird's location and another behavioral question: Where was it exactly? Was it alone? She had seen a solitary bird perched on a fence post along the road leading up to the garden.

At that point, I was skeptical that the bird had actually been a junco. I thought it more likely to have been an Eastern Phoebe. The phoebe and the junco have similar coloration—both are dark gray above and white on the belly. They aren't identical in color or shade, but if you're trying to identify one using only color as a clue, it's possible to confuse them. In other ways, they are very different, particularly in terms of location and behavior. And these details are much easier to observe than plumage.

One time, my mother called me for some natural history assistance. She lives in southern Arizona and had gone to a magnificent birding spot south of Tucson. She's not a birder; she was there just to walk and enjoy a little nature, but she did have an exciting sighting. She saw "a black bird sitting in a tree and sounding like a chicken." As ludicrous as this description sounds (sorry, Mom), it's actually quite informative. She told me exactly where the bird was and what it was doing. After some light interrogation, I found out that the bird was big (like a chicken) and was just sitting in the tree making funny sounds. Since one doesn't usually find chickens under these conditions, I'm pretty sure that what she saw was a raven. Ravens live in that area, they're large and black, they often sit in trees, and they're noteworthy for their varied vocabulary.

Where it is and what it's doing can identify a subject as readily as its appearance can. This principle applies to any living thing, including mammals and their tracks, trees, and wildflowers. Although location, behavior, and appearance all contribute to a subject's identification, location and behavior are easier to observe in the moment. Knowing this information when going through your field guide will help you make accurate identifications, and it will help you build a base of knowledge and understanding of natural history that usually comes only with years of experience. Pretty soon, you'll be the natural history expert deciphering all your friends' and family's sightings.

1

Getting Started

This book has one core message: Look at the big picture. You do this by asking the right questions: Where is it? What is it doing? How is it shaped? With these questions, you can establish a dialogue between your field experiences and your field guides, which ensures that you'll get the most out of both. Asking the big-picture questions will build your ability to think ecologically, to understand how form, function, and environment influence the survival of every living creature and shape the world around you.

The practical side of this process begins by becoming familiar with what lives in your area. Ideally, you should know the primary ecological communities in your region and the common plants, birds, and other animals in each. With that knowledge, you will be prepared for whatever you might see in the field and how to identify it. This may sound like a daunting task, but there is plenty of help available (see chapter 6). For example, the Peterson field guide series will provide all this information and more. In addition, John C. Kricher has authored several field guides dedicated to the forests of eastern and western North America (e.g., *Peterson Field Guide to the Ecology of California Forests*). These regional guides describe the major plant communities and the common plants and animals of each. They also provide short descriptive essays on significant ecological processes and patterns. After thirty minutes with such a guide, you will know the plants, birds, and mammals you are most likely to observe during your rambles.

Once you know what's in your area, you need to consider how you'll know it when you see it. Begin by determining what to look for, and then start narrowing in on where to look for it. At first, pick just a few species to concentrate on. Look over the species information as well as that pertaining to their families. Remember that this information is both explicitly written in the descriptions and implicit in the illustrations. The process is only slightly different whether you are interested in trees or mammal tracks. With trees, you might end up concentrating more on the particular details of identification. With mammals, you might devote a little more energy to understanding the ecology of the species and thinking about how those behaviors might play out in the area you like to visit: Where would foxes hunt for small mammals? Where would a bobcat den? What areas offer good bedding or feeding opportunities for deer?

Take every possible opportunity to run this information and these images through your senses. Don't pass up the chance to look closely or broadly at familiar things. I have known people who followed a robin through the woods for an hour trying unsuccessfully to identify it because it never presented its orange breast—the only thing they knew to look for. You can learn a lot from watching robins and sparrows, tracking your own dog or cat and watching it move, and looking over the plants growing in your yard. There is always something more that can be learned about any living thing. The mystery will never be completely solved. Just as immersion is the best way to learn a new language, immersion is the best way to assimilate the principles and ideas discussed in this book. You want to get to the point where you can feel them in your gut instead of just thinking about them.

Preparing for the field ahead of time is both extremely helpful and very easy. Keep your field guides handy and spend a few minutes looking through them each day. Mark the pages of the species you're particularly interested in identifying so that you can flip right to them. Your goal is to prime your mind and your senses. It's difficult for the mind to recognize something new and foreign. For example, you stand a much better chance of actually seeing rabbit feeding sign if you've seen it before (in your field guide). You will be astounded at how abundant such sign suddenly becomes once you know how to see it. Of course, the sign was there all along. But once your mind changes—once it has a search image—what was previously invisible becomes obvious. It's miraculous.

Years ago, I had the opportunity to realize a lifelong dream and spend a month in southern Africa. I imagined traveling through the savannas of northern Botswana surrounded by all that fantastic wildlife. But I was afraid of missing something good if I had to flip through a field guide to find out what kind of antelope I was looking at, so I decided to do a little preparation before the trip. I knew I couldn't learn everything, so I concentrated on the mammals I could expect to see or track, the most common birds, and the few trees that were characteristic of the region's habitats. Using only guides that were easily available, I studied the different ecosystems. The National Audubon Society's _Field Guide to African Wildlife_ and the World Wildlife Fund's Web site had descriptions that allowed me to learn the dominant species of tree. A small tree guide that I bought over the Internet showed me what mopane and brachystegia trees looked like. I was familiar with most of the large and carnivorous mammals from a lifetime of books and TV, but I studied my field guide and annotated every species of medium to large mammal that I might see. For each of these, using my field guide and the _Guide to the Behavior of African Animals_, I made a note card that included a description and drawing of the identifying field marks and key behaviors I might observe. For birds and for everything else, I browsed through the field guide often, noticing family characteristics and letting the images sink into my brain. Being familiar with bird families in a variety of habitats at home, I knew what to expect from the thrushes, starlings, weaver finches, and such. For the unfamiliar families, a little time spent imagining what their shapes told me about their behaviors and a trip to the library to consult _Birds of the World_ provided some depth to go with the pictures.

It wasn't hard work at all. It took a little time each day for a week or so before the trip—time that I would have spent excitedly imagining my upcoming journey anyway.

Ultimately, the payoff was tremendous. There were several highlights: One was realizing that African Hornbills act quite a bit like Blue Jays and Scrub Jays here at home. It was a profound feeling to look at a bird thousands of miles from my home and to feel so familiar with it. I could identify many of the other birds I saw almost immediately, having seen their pictures beforehand.

Ultimately, being grounded in the ecological patterns underlying basic natural history turned my African trip from a beautiful encounter with a parade of interesting wildlife into a thrilling experience that had personal and profound resonance. That trip brought home the value of approaching natural history from an ecological perspective. Seeing a part of Africa in those terms, I saw my own home in a new way. I saw that the habitat, behavior, and form of each organism are links to its wider community. A giraffe browsing in Camel-thorn Acacia was full of silent meaning in terms of the proportions of the giraffe's legs and the relation of that tree to the acacias of the southwestern United States. By lifting my mind from the simple question of "What is it?" and asking broader questions of the surrounding land, I could deeply appreciate the plants and animals as I got to know them and allowed myself to be introduced to new levels of excitement and mystery.

On your own journey, there's no hurry. Work on the common and abundant species first, and wring them for information.

2

Birds

At this point, you've already spent time with your field guide getting to know the birds that you're likely to encounter. You should have a good idea of when you're likely to see them, and in which habitats; their key behaviors; and how to distinguish them from closely related and similar-looking species. Lots of great birders take their guides with them into the field, but I'm more of a general naturalist than a dyed-in-the-wool birder. Faced with the prospect of taking six or more guides with me into the field, I choose to take none. In the field I concentrate on observations, often taking notes on a small pad. This forces me to spend lots of time with the books at home. Ultimately, spending time paging through your guides and imagining encounters with those birds are the best things you can do to improve your birding skills.

I recommend that you start birding without binoculars. At first, you just need to be able to spot birds—birds that quietly sneak off into the brush or zip into distant trees as you approach. The more birds you see, the more you will identify, so try to see lots of birds. Once you start to get the hang of seeing the birds, begin noticing the landscape and the birds' behaviors. Keep your mind and your eyes wide open to changes in habitat; see where the birds are within the habitat and how they act. Spend some time, wherever you are, observing bird behavior. My memories of watching House Sparrow mothers feed their fledgling young at a bus stop in New Jersey are just as precious as my memory of going to that one magical spot to glimpse some exotic species and check it off my list. Due attention to the familiar will build your skills and usher in new mysteries.

The Situation

There is a park in southern California that I used to visit almost every day when I was really learning my birds. I had been interested in natural history for a while, but I was channeling a lot of energy into building my skills as a naturalist. Let's suppose that you are walking through this park along the Creek Trail, which runs along a small creek in a wooded ravine. The trail starts off open to your right, but ahead the trees close in and cover both sides of the trail.

As you near the oak canopy, you see a couple of birds up ahead. Both are on the ground in the shadows. One is to the left of the trail near some trees and brush, and the other is a little deeper in the woods under the trees to the right. You stop when you see them and watch for a few moments. You want to get a better look, but as you approach, they both fly away. All you could see for sure was that they were both medium sized, about the size of a robin, and both brown. The shadows made it hard to tell, but neither had

Under the shade of the oak canopy, you get a fleeting look at two ground birds.

any obvious or bold markings. You're pretty sure that they were two different species, however, because one seemed to have a longer tail and was a little lighter color than the other.

In the moment that you see a bird, you strive to observe all you can, but there is often little time. Sometimes there are obvious details of appearance that make identification easy, but it takes practice to see them. In this case, you didn't see anything that would distinguish one bird from another. Given that you saw little of the two birds' plumage and field marks, even if you could find some possible

The birds are partly obscured by distance, shade, and vegetation.

matches by flipping through every page in your field guide, you still couldn't be confident of an identification. There will always be sightings that stump you or leave you feeling a little confused, but let's look at this situation again. Was it really so ambiguous? What else could you have noticed?

Taking a Closer Look

It's important to notice where the birds are within the habitat, or the natural setting where they live. I call this location within the habitat the "microhabitat." With birds, this generally refers to where they are in relation to the ground and what they are perching on. Since they can fly, birds' micro-habitat can be anywhere from on the ground to thousands of feet up in the air.

Most birds are observed when they are foraging, so we can assume that both the birds you saw are ground feeders, but they were doing so differently. The first bird scratched in the leaves with its feet. It used an odd double-scratch technique, like short foot-dragging hops backward. The other bird scooted along by running, one foot in front of the other, intermittently picking through the leaves with its beak. The manner of the first bird was what I call high-strung; its movements were sharp and jerky. The other bird was more fluid, almost sneaky. The posture of the two birds was similar, generally stooped forward. But the first bird held its tail and often its head up a bit, whereas the second bird's tail was angled down and it kept its head hunched down, at least while it was looking for food.

This may seem like too much to have noticed with such a brief glimpse, but the more you practice paying attention, the more you'll see. But how is this useful? You can't look up behavior in a field guide. The point is, behavior can provide other information that will help identify these birds from a book.

For instance, we are guessing that these birds are ground feeders based on microhabitat and behavior. Micro-habitats are not random; they depend on where these birds have to be to find the right food. For instance, only a few types of birds have the traits necessary to make their livings on the trunks of trees. Each has a particular mix of physical form and behavior that allows it to exploit tree trunks for survival. Woodpeckers have pecking bills; strong, grasping feet; and stiff tails that act like kickstands, allowing them to support themselves on tree trunks and limbs and dig out insects for food. Nuthatches and creepers also feed on trunks and have their own unique traits that allow them to do so. So any bird on a tree trunk is a woodpecker, a nuthatch, or a creeper. The behavior of these three kinds of birds allows you to distinguish among them at great distances. Woodpeckers feed head-up, working their way upward as they go. Nuthatches feed head-down and work their way from the tops of trees to the bottoms. Creepers work their way upward but move stealthily, hugging the tree closely, whereas woodpeckers jut out and move about noticeably. The human eye registers movement and form before it registers color, so by the time you see the plumage, your job is narrowed down to identifying the species of woodpecker, creeper, or nuthatch. Since we have a sense of what is available to eat on the ground here—seeds and invertebrates—we should be able to make some guesses about the birds' beaks. The beak is the primary tool for foraging. It has other functions, such as grooming feathers, but feeding ecology has a major influence on the form of the beak. Even though both birds you saw are ground feeders, I would guess that they have different beaks based on their different foraging behaviors.

Woodpecker beaks are stout, straight, and sharp for pecking into wood. Nuthatches have fine, straight, sharp bills that are good for picking insects and spiders from bark crevices and are capable of hacking into tough seeds and nuts. Creepers move slowly up trees and limbs using their fine, downward-curving bills to pluck bugs from the bark.

Microhabitat and behavior clearly identify woodpeckers, nuthatches, and creepers as trunk feeders. Broad arrows show flight paths. Small arrows show trunk foraging paths.

In addition to insect-eating bills like these, there are beaks designed for eating every other kind of available food.

Suppose you were a bird picking through leaves to find your food. Would you want a long beak or a short beak? Consider the people who pick up trash in parks and on roadsides. They usually carry a pincerlike grabber with a 3-foot handle. Imagine trying to pick up trash with a pair of pliers. If you had to use pliers, you might change your tactics. Maybe instead of picking up each piece of trash individually, you would kick a bunch of it together in a pile and then pick it up all at once.

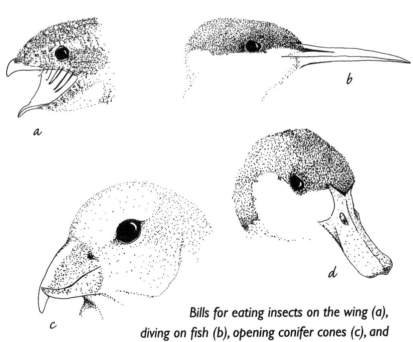

Bills for eating insects on the wing (a), diving on fish (b), opening conifer cones (c), and dabbling in pond mud (d).

These birds (their ancestors, actually) have had to grapple with these same issues of effort and efficiency. Because of this, I would guess that the bird picking through the debris with its beak has a longer beak than the other bird. But why would a bird feeding in debris have a short beak at all? The answer has to do with leverage. A 3-foot-long trash grabber is good for picking up litter, but I would rather have pliers for loosening a nut on my car—or for cracking a nut, for that matter. Many ground-feeding birds that eat seeds have short, stout bills like pliers that allow them to crack or husk hard seeds. If your preferred food was seeds, you would be better off with a stout, seed-cracker bill. And if you had a bill like that, you probably wouldn't use it to dig through leaves; you would use your feet, like a chicken. It's efficient, and it's the behavior that fits the tool. I would guess that the longer-billed bird probably doesn't eat seeds, or at least not as its main diet. It probably eats invertebrates, using its longer, tweezer-like bill to grab and hold bugs hiding in the leaves.

The other thing you saw both birds do was fly. Both birds had a fluttery flight. The scratcher didn't fly far, just farther along the trail. If you had kept walking, you probably would have seen it again. The bill picker, when it flushed, flew over the low ridge to the left and out of sight; it seemed to be headed to another patch of woods about 50 yards away. It flew low and straight in an even line. The manner, how readily, and where a bird flies to are clues about its ecology and its identity. Maybe next time you'll only need to see the trajectory of a distant bird's flight to accurately identify it. This is exactly what experienced birders do when they seem to magically identify birds from mere glimpses.

Taking a Broader Look

Recall the moment that you first saw the birds. Just by noticing them, you gathered critical information about their identities. The location of the sighting eliminates all those birds whose ranges and habitats don't include that area. This particular park is just east of a sharp point sticking out into the Pacific above the westward sweep of the southern California coast. It is on the seaward edge of some high, chaparral-covered mountains.

The majority of California is hot and dry and could never naturally support the palm trees and exotic tropical plants associated with the Golden State. Much of central and southern California is dominated by drought-resistant oak woodlands and a scrub woodland called chaparral. Lack of moisture limits chaparral to a profusion of prickly, scratchy shrubs that form an almost impenetrable thicket spreading over the poor, rocky soil. In this park, oak woods fill the creek bottoms between chaparral-covered hills. Open fields consisting of dry meadows maintained by mowing add some diversity to the landscape.

So, you know that these birds include southern California in their ranges. You also know that they can tolerate the chaparral habitat. Species ranges are influenced by the extremes of climate, particularly temperature, and the kind of ecosystem. Some birds suited to woodland ecosystems could never survive in a desert either because they couldn't find the food (and water) they need or because the heat itself would prove fatal. Each species has to be able to find

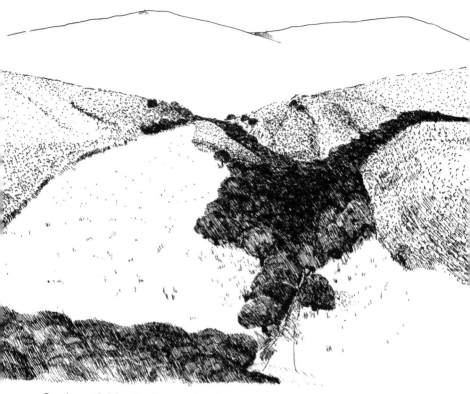

Southern California chaparral, oak woodland, and dry meadow. The Creek Trail can be seen entering the oaks at the bottom of the picture, just right of center.

the right food, water, and shelter and, for residents, suitable nesting sites and materials. The particular ecosystems that meet these needs describe the habitat that a species can occupy. Predators, birds, and other animals competing for the same foods can influence a bird's habitat as well. It's also important to consider the season of the sighting, since some birds are present in their North American ranges for only part of the year—something that is clearly noted in good field guides.

You know that these two birds can inhabit oak woods and chaparral and perhaps other habitats as well. In a field guide covering all of North America, there are over nine hundred species listed. A little over two hundred species are found on land in this part of California and less than half of those live in dry, wooded, or brushy areas like these. So, in that first instant of the sighting, you gained critical information for making the identification. You'll definitely want to file it away under this bird's name when you get to that.

Taking a Look at the Bird Itself

Finally, what did the bird actually look like? In reality, your mind processes all this information together, but in terms of imposing a logical pattern and structure on your observations, save these details for last. When observing birds, look at their component shapes: beak, wings, tail, and even feet, if possible. These are the characteristics by which ornithologists define species, not coloration. You should be able to note these features fairly quickly when they're visible, and you'll still be able to notice the plumage colors and other aspects. The above list of possible species can be reduced to five or six based on size and shape.

Note the overall size of the bird. We called the birds in this example robin sized, denoting a medium-sized bird. As you learn a few birds, you can use them as relative sizes, such as warbler and crow sized. This makes it easy to remember and to communicate to others. Your field guide is the best teacher of which details deserve attention—things such as wing bars, mustachial lines, and eye lines. First, spend some time with the "bird topography" diagram somewhere in the front of your guide so that you'll know what the various parts are called. Make sure that you're familiar with these features, because they are the basis of the species descriptions you will ultimately be relying on. Eventually, you'll begin to see family patterns emerge. For instance, wing bars are important when differentiating sparrows but not tanagers.

So far, we've been able to mine quite a bit of information from that quick sighting, although the details of appearance are still largely lacking. We've been engaging in a dialogue with the object of our attention, but that object isn't just the bird; it's the bird and landscape, the bird as it evolved and continues to survive as part of a dynamic community. We're going to get to the names of these birds eventually. But your goal should not be just the name; it should be to know the thing for which the name is a symbol.

Names are the keys to unlocking the volumes of experience and information that others have collected in books and images. But that information will have meaning only if those names are invested in a rich impression of the bird as a living being interacting with a complex ecological community. At this point, we've made the observations and drawn what conclusions we can. Now it's time to go to the field guide.

Making the Identification

The ultimate objective when using a field guide for identification is to find a picture that looks just like what you saw. One of my primary goals is to save you the tedium of flipping through every page in your guide to find a match. The result of the previous steps—looking at what the bird is doing and where it is and then thinking about its physical features—can narrow your search and deepen your knowledge.

Many guides also include a little information on microhabitat in the picture. In my guide, ground-feeding birds are pictured on the ground in appropriate settings, shorebirds are on rocks or sand, woodpeckers are on trees, and sparrows are on the ground or in low vegetation. Even the species of trees included in the drawings are appropriate to the bird species' range. When you look at the picture, you are seeing the posture, structure, and appearance of the birds, plus their microhabitat.

If you flip through your guide looking for the two birds observed—the scratcher and the bill picker—you'll notice that there are large sections filled with birds that look nothing like them. All the gulls and terns are grouped together, as are the ducks and geese, owls, and hummingbirds. Thus, you can essentially disregard most of the book.

Many field guides are arranged phylogenetically, which means that the families are depicted in the order in which they evolved. For example, the loon family has been around the longest of all modern birds, so it comes first. The finch family was the most recent on the scene, so it comes last. So if you know the family of the bird you're looking for, you can narrow your search. The good news is that you already know a number of bird families, because the common terms for birds usually correspond to their family names. For example, in a field guide, the birds we collectively call owls will be located together as a family, with the individual owl species displayed on consecutive pages. Once you're familiar with the key characteristics of a family, it's not hard to categorize a new species on the first try. Most field guides help by giving brief descriptions of family characteristics at the beginning of each section. The best way to familiarize yourself with bird families is to make the family a vital part of the basic information you learn about any bird you identify in the field or read about in a book.

Based on our interpretation of the behaviors observed, the birds seen along the Creek Trail are in two different families. Start by flipping through the field guide and looking not necessarily for the specific bird but for a family of birds that resembles what you saw. Read the family descriptions as you do this. Once you find the probable family, search for a bird that matches not just the appearance but also the range and habitat of what you saw. Look at the graphics *and* read the text. Flycatcher bills might look right, but the description will tell you that flycatchers generally hunt insects in the air from an exposed perch, which is clearly not what you saw.

The bill picker likely has a longish bill that is straight or down-curved, the typical pattern for ground-feeding, insect-eating birds. As you go through your guide, thinking about tails and bills, a number of possibilities will catch your eye, but most will not stand up to scrutiny. A liberal list for the bill picker might be Mourning Dove, Hermit Thrush, California Thrasher, and maybe even Wrentit.

The Mourning Dove is long and low with a long tail. Mourning Doves feed on the ground and have longish bills. The Hermit Thrush is a ground feeder that can be found in the area, but it has a stubby tail, and the illustrated posture is very upright. The Wrentit has the right body

Hermit Thrush (a), Mourning Dove (b), Wrentit (c), and California Thrasher (d).

shape and dimensions, and it is a chaparral bird. It's rather small, though, unless we overestimated the size of the bird sighted. Finally, the thrasher looks right in body structure and dimension and has the ideal bill for the foraging behavior we observed.

A simple reference that provides a little more natural history than the typical field guide would likely clarify the picture. Of all the birds listed, only the California Thrasher is uniformly dark brown, has a long tail, picks through leaf litter with its bill ("thrashing"), and is common in chaparral. This is exactly why a good natural history reference is an important tool for building your skills in the field. It's also helpful to look at the photos or paintings of birds in several guides, seeing them in different poses.

The first thrasher I ever identified was a California Thrasher in just this situation. What clinched it for me was knowing that thrashers "thrash" and having an impression of their long shapes from time spent poring over a field guide. After the bird flew off, I followed it over the hill, found it again (I heard it in the leaves), and snuck up for a closer view. I just needed a good look at that bill to positively identify the bird in the guide. Only much later was I able to watch a few of them closely enough to pick up all their other field marks.

Working on identifying the scratcher, only the emberizid, cardinal, and finch families exhibit the ideal "conical" seed-cracking beak we presume that it has. However, most of the species in these families are small, colorful, or found

Drab-colored and common in chaparral-covered foothills, the California Thrasher uses its large, curved bill to flip leaf litter aside as it forages on the ground.

Some southern California members of the family **Emberizidae**—*the sparrows and allies. Junco (a), Rufous-capped Sparrow (b), California Towhee (c), Spotted Towhee (d).*

outside of this location. The most likely matches are among the emberizids—the sparrows and allies. These birds are a little more similar than the short list for the thrasher. Identifying this bird will ultimately depend on plumage color and pattern, because all these birds fit the structural, range, and habitat criteria. If we can be sure that it was a medium-sized bird that lacked streaking and patterning, that leaves only the California Towhee with the necessary traits. In order to settle on a single bird, you need to have a sense of why it couldn't have been something else.

Note that if you had seen a smaller, streaky bird in that same scenario, your job would have been much harder. Species identification often rests on the details, and in those cases, you may not walk away from a sighting with a positive identification. You would, however, be much better prepared to get it right the next time.

Now you know the names of the birds you saw, but that's just the beginning. When you visit that spot again and see a bird in the shadows, you might think, "That bird sure isn't acting like a California Towhee." Even better, now you can read up on these birds in your field guide and other resources. If you do, you'll learn—like I did, after my first sighting—that the California Towhee commonly gives a metallic *chink!* as a call note. The next time I was out for a walk, my mind suddenly registered that I had been hearing these notes almost constantly without even realizing it.

Brownish overall and resident in chaparral, the California Towhee forages mostly on the ground, sometimes scratching among the leaf litter.

Suddenly I was identifying California Towhees everywhere simply by this sound and a quick rustle in the brush.

Birding by Ear

Birdsong and other vocalizations are valuable tools for birders. In addition to songs, many birds make distinctive calls throughout the year that are fantastic aids for identification. Using vocalizations is easiest when you prepare ahead of time. Choose a few common species on which to concentrate, and review and learn their songs and calls before going into the field. When you're adept at recognizing those first few, tackle a few more.

There are some good resources for songs and calls, but the best way to learn birdsong is to use those resources to make your own recordings. For example, if you want to learn the robin, record its vocalizations from a commercial tape or CD several times over. Then do another repetitive recording for, say, the mockingbird. When you listen to the recording, you'll hear the robin song five or six times in a row, followed by similar repetitions of the mockingbird. You can do four or five species this way. This will familiarize you with their songs much faster than if you simply listened to an entire CD of all the birds in the east or west over and over.

A friend of mine spent one summer surveying breeding birds in his hometown as part of a statewide research project. He admitted that he had to relearn all the songs each year because, for some reason, they never stuck with him. In addition to doing some good focused preparation of the sort mentioned above, he shared a new technique that I hadn't thought of. He carries an iPod into the field so that he can play through the candidate songs on site and compare them to the actual songster. The key to this handy trick is that he has a base of knowledge about the songs of certain families or groups of species, making his in-the-field recording search narrow and efficient.

Looking Deeper

Approaching your field observations from an ecological perspective prepares you to see patterns that were previously invisible. Your field guide can tell you how things look. I want you to think beyond mere appearances—in terms of the underlying patterns of ecological life. Form, function, and environment are interacting parts of a whole organism. As you apply this perspective, you will learn to recognize a bird's family or even subfamily at the first sighting. As you saw, simply noticing where the bird is in the habitat can imply family through traits such as feeding behavior or beak shape.

I once asked myself why so many chaparral birds have long tails. There seemed to be a pattern in the wings of many species too. Scrub Jays, for example, have long tails and broad, stubby wings that make a fluttery sound when they fly. Why this shape? This is the question I began carrying in my head as I walked and watched. It was a simple question, but it deepened the impact of my daily observations.

One day I followed the Creek Trail into the high meadow. I was sitting in the stubble of the recently mowed field watching nothing in particular when I saw a Red-tailed Hawk soaring above me. As I watched, another bird came up over the lip of the hill beside me. This second

A Cooper's Hawk flaps to a new perch while a Red-tailed Hawk soars overhead.

hawk shot right over my head about 20 feet off the ground. I had a great view of it as it sailed away and disappeared deep into the opposite wood line. I knew what kinds of hawks might be in the area, and I had seen enough to be sure that it was a Cooper's Hawk that shot over my head. Seeing that Cooper's Hawk answered my question about why I was seeing so many birds with long tails.

A Red-tailed Hawk hunts by soaring high above the ground and looking down for prey. It spends many hours each day circling and drifting without flapping its wings. When a redtail soars, it spreads its long, broad wings and flares its tail into a short wedge. It makes its body into a wide paraglider, allowing it to catch rising currents of warm air and ride them all day long. If you watch a redtail soar in unstable air, its tail is constantly angling this way and that, balancing the airflow over its body. The tail is the steering mechanism, and the wings provide the lift. The spread of the primary feathers on the ends of the wings decreases drag and lets the hawk soar at very slow speeds without stalling and falling from the sky. Redtails are often seen hunting from perches along highways. Whether hunting or roosting, they often perch in the uppermost part of a tree for better access to their primary element, the open sky. Redtails rise from their roosts slowly, with heavy wing beats. Those long, broad wings that are so excellent for soaring are tiresome to flap—a trade-off in efficiency between soaring and active flying.

In contrast, a Cooper's Hawk has short wings. It spends less time soaring, preferring to hunt from a roost within the woods. The Cooper's Hawk perches under the upper canopy and watches for prey, usually small birds, which are pursued and captured in the air. Its short, broad wings are more efficient for flapping than a redtail's are. They catch a lot of air, allowing the Cooper's to fly quickly and with great agility. The long tail gives it even more power in its maneuvering, a critical capability for aerial pursuit in canopied woodlands.

All hawks and their close relatives have the same basic features—grasping talons, tearing beaks, flying wings, and steering tails—but in each species, those features are molded to suit a particular prey and habitat. The Cooper's Hawk is a hawk built in the bird-chasing woodland mold. The Red-tailed Hawk soars high over open country as it hunts for small rodents and rabbits. The American Kestrel,

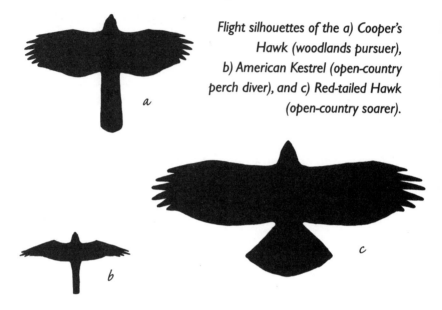

Flight silhouettes of the a) Cooper's Hawk (woodlands pursuer), b) American Kestrel (open-country perch diver), and c) Red-tailed Hawk (open-country soarer).

a small falcon, hunts from an exposed perch in open territory. It doesn't need broad wings or a long tail for bursts of speed and maneuverability, but it must be able to drop quickly from a perch when it spots a grasshopper. Accordingly, kestrels have narrow, pointed wings.

Members of the flycatcher family are calm, stately birds. They usually sit on mid- to high-elevation perches from which they fly out and catch insects on the wing. Their bills are broad at the base, open wide, and have "whiskers" and a hooked tip to help catch and hold prey. Warblers are small, often brightly colored, "nervous" birds that pick soft insects off the foliage of trees and bushes with their small pointed beaks. Sparrows generally have stout bills, thick from top to bottom, for leverage in cracking seeds. They are found mostly on the ground and often in flocks.

Microhabitat can provide clues to how a bird might look or act. Here, a Western Wood Peewee (a), an Orange-crowned Warbler (b), and a Golden-crowned Sparrow (c) are shown at the relative heights where they are seen in oak woodlands or chaparral.

These aren't hard-and-fast rules, but they are valuable. Even if you can say that a bird is warblerlike, you are well on your way to identifying its family and maybe even the bird itself—and you are learning a deeper story about the living landscape. Ecological and family traits give you a place to start. Then you can search for the details that distinguish one species or another within that group. Those field marks illustrated in your field guide that used to seem like an endless parade of obscure details will now fit easily into a rich and expanding picture of birds and bird life.

3

Mammals and Their Tracks

Tracking is a language, one in which the words are the marks left by animals during the course of their daily lives. When an animal moves across the land, it isn't moving at random any more than these letters are arranged randomly on the page. The signs are formed according to laws of ecology, adaptation, and survival, and they are infused with meaning. By reading the pattern and the character of an animal's movement through the woods, you can learn the language of its survival, which, in the deepest sense, is its identity.

Great trackers say that the key to successful tracking is knowing what to look for and where to look for it. With tracking, the first skill you need to acquire is the ability to notice tracks and sign. Immerse yourself in both a mammal guide and a tracking guide. To expand the language analogy: A tracking guide is a vocabulary list, but a mammal guide shows you how to put the words together in a meaningful way. As you look at what makes a rabbit a rabbit and not a squirrel, look at the typical tracks and sign for both rabbits and squirrels. This will make you more likely to see some of the signs that you've been overlooking and help you unravel the story behind new signs that you've never seen before.

As a tracker, you're particularly interested in how animals move, so avail yourself of every opportunity to watch animals on TV, in the zoo, or in the wild. Start by learning the habits of common mammals and by watching domesticated animals for what they can teach you about animal movement. As you are out exploring, you'll learn all the tracks and sign in time, but it is your knowledge of the animal, its body, and its ecology that will make the difference at the end of the day.

The Situation

One fine winter day, we are taking a walk through the Vermont woods. There is nearly 2 feet of light snow on the ground. We end up heading down into the fair-sized valley of a small brook. On the way, we come across some tracks.

Most people walk right up and look down inside tracks—a reasonable reaction. They're looking for that nice footprint, one that matches the black-and-white illustrations in their field guides. Clear track images are what most tracking guides specialize in, especially the ones aimed at beginners.

But we're out of luck. These tracks were made during the cold snap after the snow fell. The new snow hadn't firmed up yet, so it spilled all over when the tracks were made. We can't see any foot details in these tracks. Fortunately, the structure of the foot and footprint is just one part

In the winter woods,
we come across this trail.

of a bigger picture that can lead to the identity of the track maker. Unless it's snowing as you're tracking, you can take your time, because the tracks aren't going anywhere.

Taking a Closer Look

It's easy to notice that the tracks fall in a regular pattern. Trail patterns like this are the result of the animal's method of movement, or gait. Human gaits include walking and hopping, which, as you can probably imagine, make very different tracks. The pattern of the tracks we've found can be described as alternating, since they appear to alternate back and forth across an imaginary centerline. This pattern is associated with walking and trotting gaits.

Every animal has certain preferred gaits that are comfortable and efficient, given its body structure and other

Because of the deep snow,
the details of the tracks are not visible.

ecological necessities. Most of the tracks we see reflect the preferred gait, indicating some animals over others. Some tracking guides include excellent descriptions of different gaits and their associated patterns; some guides even use these patterns as a key to help you make a short list of likely species. A basic understanding of gaits gives you a place to begin interpreting trail patterns for information about the size, shape, and behavior of your quarry.

First, think about the trail pattern of a four-legged animal in simple, physical terms. You would make a pattern like the one we've found in the snow if you were crawling on all fours and putting your knees down in the tracks made by your hands. As long as you're moving in a walk so that your knees are registering directly in your hand prints, two strides is roughly the length of your torso. Give it a try. Being able to mimic different gaits is a huge asset when tracking. The strides in this trail are about 16 inches, so we're looking at a torso of about 32 inches. This is just a rule of thumb, something to give you a rough estimate of the size of the animal that made the tracks.

The depth of the prints is important. Don't lament that the snow contributed to hiding the footprint. Consider that squirrel tracks and moose tracks have a superficial resemblance as they are drawn in many guides. But because a moose weighs thousands of times more than a squirrel, it

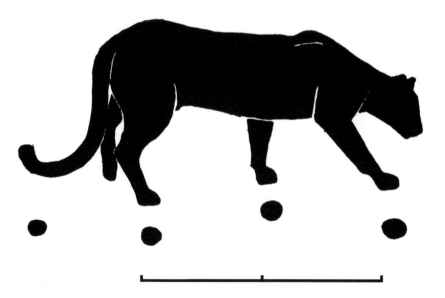

Two strides from one heel to the next in a basic walking gait are roughly equal to the animal's torso length.

sinks 3 feet or more into snow that a squirrel barely leaves an impression in. You have to consider the hardness of the snow as well, but generally, deep tracks mean a heavy animal. If an animal is sinking in the snow, its belly may drag. With an alternating pattern like this, an absence of belly drags means that the animal's legs are longer than the depth of the tracks in the snow. For example, porcupines have short legs, so in this snow, their trails would look like troughs with footprints down inside them, and you would be able to see the brushing of the belly across the tops of the tracks. (Once, after 2 feet of light snow fell overnight, the snow was deeper than the backs of the porcupines and they actually made tunnels as they walked from tree to tree.) In the trail we found, there are drag marks of the feet between the tracks, but no body marks. Therefore, we can conclude that these are the tracks of a large animal with a long torso and long legs. Now we want to step back, so to speak, and look at how the trail interacts with the land. Every animal has a thorough understanding of the landscape it inhabits and uses it according to its needs, strengths, and vulnerabilities.

Taking a Broader Look

Look again at the trail. It doesn't move in a straight line from the swamp; it's crooked, cutting it back and forth. The turns are abrupt, something other than just meanders. The woods are pretty open here, and an animal could pass through in a nearly straight line if it wanted to. Although there is always an element of mystery to an animal's actions, we can be sure that it isn't moving randomly. Since walking in deep snow requires a lot of energy, it would be

*From the swampy
area, the trail goes up into the hemlock grove.*

foolish in this harsh season to be wandering around aim-lessly (except for those of us who are assured of a hot meal and a warm bed when we get home).

What is drawing it back and forth? At each of these turns is a small shrub or low-hanging branch of a larger tree. What is this animal after? Food is always a good bet as a motive. Look over the shrubs with an eye toward what might have been eaten. There are no leaves or fruit at this time of year, but all the shrubs have branches whose ends were bitten off. Some of the bitten branches are nearly 4 feet off the ground. This animal was browsing, feeding on twigs and buds, as it moved, and it was reaching quite high up.

The browsed branches are roughly bitten off.

Judging by how the trail moves toward and away from these shrubs, we can conclude that the animal came up out of the swampy thickets by the creek and into the hemlock woods. If determining the direction of travel is difficult, walk around a bit and use your own footprints as a reference. So far, we know that we are tracking a large animal that browses, feeding on twigs. The trail also suggests that this animal might have a particular preference for swampy or coniferous microhabitats, but we would have to trail it longer to be sure. Large animals have large ranges, so they can move through a lot of different habitats during their travels. They definitely have preferences that you can discover, but they're not always apparent from a short section of trail.

In deep, fluffy snow a red squirrel bound can look like a weasel bound. In such light snow, the squirrel wouldn't overstep its front feet with its hind feet; it would put the hind feet down right where the front feet were—which is how a weasel moves. The effect is a pattern consisting of two holes, or two holes blending into one, in the loose snow. This happens frequently throughout the winter and can stump someone who is relying solely on ideal images from a track guide. You won't be tricked, however, if you look at where the animal is going and what it is doing. Weasels and squirrels are different in form and function, and those differences will be apparent if you take in the broader scene of the tracks within the landscape.

The same principles apply to deer and other large animals. Every magazine on deer hunting has an article on how to read the land in order to predict where the big bucks will be. The same can be done for any animal that people hunt. My favorite example in Vermont, where I live, involves the differences between foxes and coyotes. Red foxes tend to be found closer to human habitation than coyotes are. Foxes can be found in the woods as well, but they don't travel too far into the woods before coming out to investigate the open fields and pastures. Coyotes use the woods more exclusively. This is a pattern I discovered simply by tracking these animals when I moved to the area, but I subsequently found that there is some scientific research to back up my observation. Coyotes, perhaps because people hunt them more aggressively than they do foxes, tend to keep space between themselves and the surrounding farms. Foxes may enjoy a little protection from coyotes by living in the shadow of humans. With a sense of the size and nature of the animal you're tracking, building a picture of how it is using the land can go a long way toward identifying it.

Using Your Knowledge and Field Guides

As I track, I formulate a mental list of possible species for any set of tracks I'm unsure of. As I look over the tracks, the trail, and the landscape, gathering information, I'm looking for things that will help me eliminate animals from that list. This is where field guides come in handy. Along with a good field guide to tracks, you need a good field guide to mammals. This mammal guide is your reference for the size, shape, and ecology of the animals you're tracking. It tells you about the particular habits—migration, hibernation, dates of mating—that drive the behavior and the tracks you see. Start by learning about the animals, and learning their tracks will come naturally.

A good track guide has information on the size, shape, and appearance of tracks. It should also include information on the most common trail patterns, with associated measurements of trail width and stride. Finally, it should tell you about sign other than footprints. In our case, some information about bitten-off twig ends would be useful, because even twig browsing can be distinctive. Some guides are organized by species. Others are organized by the type of sign: tracks, feeding sign, marks on vegetation, and so forth. Both have their advantages, but by formulating some educated guesses as to what animal you might be tracking beforehand, your guide will be more useful.

Most tracking guides are built around ideal images of tracks that are unique in size and shape to each species. You may occasionally find tracks that look just like them, but more often than not, you will have to use your imagination to interpret how an idealized track would be transformed on different surfaces and under different conditions, as in

Rodent Order

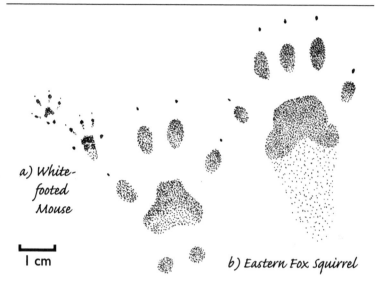

a) White-footed Mouse

1 cm

b) Eastern Fox Squirrel

Even-toed, Hoofed Order

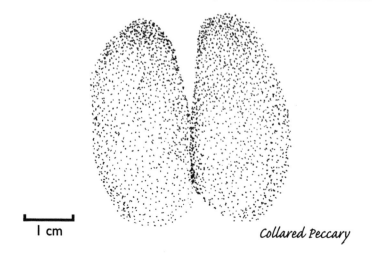

1 cm

Collared Peccary

Each order has a characteristic track form and size range.

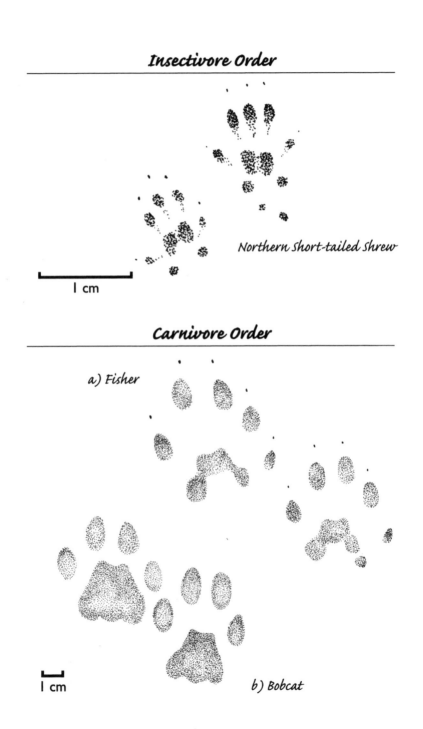

Insectivore Order

Northern Short-tailed Shrew

1 cm

Carnivore Order

a) Fisher

1 cm

b) Bobcat

the squirrel example above. This is when an overreliance on simple picture matching will let you down. Matching a clear picture to a track image is a matter of comparing length and width, the number and shape of toes, and the shape and number of other pads, claws, and such. Tracks—or, rather, the feet that make them—are similar in appearance within families. If you can recognize a dog track, you have the template for all members of the dog family: wolves, coyotes, foxes. The tracks of each member of the family have their own particular characteristics, but they all follow the same dog foot plan—four toes, nonretractile claws, small palm pad, and symmetrical, oval shape.

Making the Identification

Even if you know nothing about mammals, you can quickly narrow down the list of possibilities by skimming the orders and families in your mammal guide. As with birds, these biological classifications are shorthand for certain traits and behaviors. Body form and, to a certain extent, size, as well as eating habits, tend to be consistent within orders and even more so within families.

If you skim a good mammal guide for large browsers, you will find the order (a group of families) Artiodactyla, the animals with two-toed hooves like cows and sheep. In this case, only the deer family has members in Vermont. The two species of that family that we need to consider are the white-tailed deer and the moose, which are generally found in the same habitats but differ markedly in size. At this point, even before consulting a tracking guide, we can be reasonably sure that we've been tracking a white-tailed deer. Although their tracks and sign are quite similar, the tracks of the moose are much bigger, and in a walk, a short

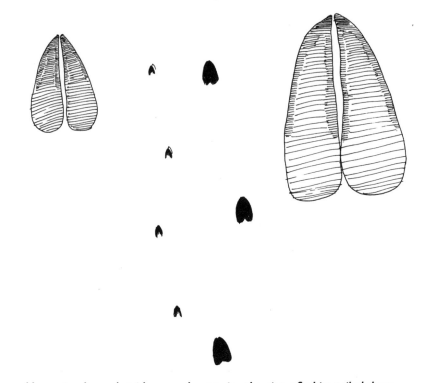

Moose tracks and strides are about twice the size of white-tailed deer tracks.

stride for a moose is generally longer than the longest deer stride. We can thus conclude that it was a white-tailed deer that walked up out of the swamp, feeding as it moved.

You don't need to know the difference between a white-tailed deer track and a mule deer track, because there are no mule deer in the East. Even where white-tailed and mule deer ranges overlap, the whitetails prefer moister habitats, and the mule deer like the drier areas. In other words, for deer, family + size + habitat = species.

What is true for deer is true for other families: Of all the species in a given family, only a small number will be found in any particular location. There are sixteen species of chipmunk in North America that are nearly identical physically. Chipmunk tracks and trails look basically like those of other members of the squirrel family, falling somewhere in the middle between small squirrels and large ones. I can recognize chipmunk sign but must refer to a mammal guide to determine which species I have found. I rely on family characteristics, size, and the big picture of range and habitat to get me past having to consider (impossibly) minute differences between such closely similar species.

Looking Deeper

Don't stop here. Push yourself beyond the name of the animal to a fuller understanding of how to track it in the future. Look for illustrations or descriptions of the feeding sign of whitetails. You'll find the same kind of browsing you saw in this example, plus a few other signs such as bark feeding and beds that you haven't seen yet. But now that you know what to look for, you're much more likely to find these other signs. Look again at the tracks and file them away in your mind. The next time, you may be able to recognize that a deer passed in deep snow from the tracks alone.

From a larger perspective, the woods in central Vermont are a mix of deciduous and coniferous trees. The greater area is described as northern hardwoods, a deciduous forest dominated here by beech, maple, and birch. Coniferous trees are sprinkled throughout but are most abundant in low, moist areas. There aren't a lot of species of large mammals in North America, so very few probably include this area in their ranges.

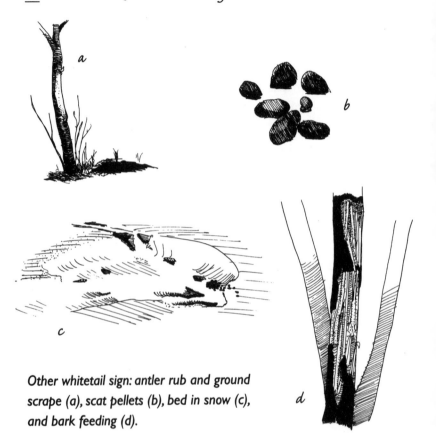

Other whitetail sign: antler rub and ground scrape (a), scat pellets (b), bed in snow (c), and bark feeding (d).

Tracking means being able to think in terms of the animal's survival strategies. We've already learned about the feeding habits and perhaps some habitat preferences of whitetails. We don't want to overlook the fact that we're tracking in winter. Cold winters mean limited food resources but higher caloric needs to maintain body temperature and move through deep snow. There are different ways for animals to cope with the rigors of a snowy northern winter. Many birds simply leave, flying south to where they will be able to find food. Insects, reptiles, and amphibians hibernate, going dormant in protected spots such as holes and burrows until spring returns. Some mammals also hibernate or slow their metabolism and sleep during long periods of cold weather. Small mammals restrict their activities to underground; the blanketing snow acts as an insulator, protecting these frail creatures from the full brunt of winter's chill. The mammals out and about leaving tracks in the dead of winter are those that are able to adjust to the sparse food, snow, and cold temperatures while remaining active aboveground.

The white-tailed deer may prefer swampy thickets and hemlock groves, but since we've only seen a small bit of trail, we can't be sure. Swamps are good habitat for shrubs and other low growth that offer food and concealment for deer. Hemlocks and other conifers intercept some of the snow that falls, so the snow cover is less deep under them. Conifers and thickets can also provide cover from the wind, which robs bodies of heat. The deer is clearly not a hibernator and needs to use the land in a very particular way to reduce the stresses of winter. It's a short step from here to the point where you can look far off into the woods, see faint suggestions of tracks, and guess that they are from deer.

Sign Tracking

In times and places where tracks are difficult to see, trackers must become familiar with the other signs of wildlife. Most tracking guides have information lumped together by species, so when you find some kind of browse or perhaps tooth marks on an acorn, you need to be able to narrow the possibilities to a few species for a quick search of the book. As with tracks, you should consider the whole picture of the sign as an ecological event. What is the habitat? Where in the habitat is the sign located? What object is the sign on? How big is the sign? What action could have made this sign?

If the earlier deer example had taken place in the summer or fall, how might it have played out? Without the snow, you wouldn't have gotten a sense of the stride or leg length, but you could still see the height of the browse and the habitat. Sometimes, even when you can't see tracks, you can make out the trail of an animal through green plants or dried leaves. This won't tell you precisely which animal passed by, but knowing where it was traveling gives you one more piece of the puzzle. This is undoubtedly more challenging, but just knowing the height that the animal can reach and that it's browsing will steer you to the right information in your field guide. With this sign, some ecological perspective, and information from your mammal guide, you can be confident that you are tracking a deer.

Seeing the Animal in the Tracks

Now let's look at a set of clear tracks and see how the ecological view can inform our tracking. Imagine that you're a zoologist from another planet and you've never seen or even heard of a bear. You're walking along and find some black bear tracks in the dust of a forest road in California or Idaho or Florida or Quebec. Just from understanding the ecology of animals and working from this track, you can discover a lot about what a bear is.

First of all, it's a big animal. Some of the tracks probably aren't much smaller than your own feet. If you look closer at the tracks, you'll see that there is a distinct difference between the front and rear tracks, but which is which? The

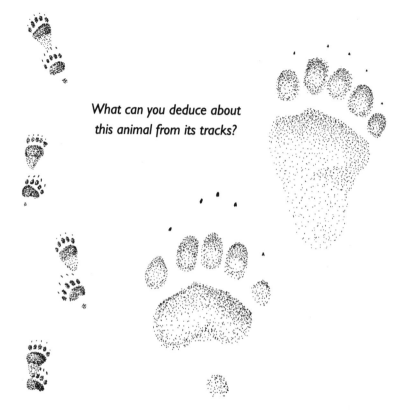

What can you deduce about this animal from its tracks?

smaller tracks have longer claws. Long claws like these are used for either digging or climbing. Cats, which use their sharp claws to catch prey, can retract their claws into sheaths on the toes to protect them, so they usually don't show up in tracks. Claws for digging are generally longer than those for grabbing, and they are most pronounced on the front feet. Therefore we can surmise that the tracks with the longer claws are the front feet, meaning that the rear feet are the larger ones.

So how big is this animal? Let's say that the walking stride is about 20 inches. Although this isn't a direct register walk (rears on top of fronts), you can use two strides, or roughly 40 inches, as a decent estimate of the body size. I would guess that if this bear were walking in a direct register, it might have a smaller stride, so 40 inches shoulder to hip may be an overestimate. With a 20-inch stride, the limbs are at least 20 inches long and probably a bit longer. But don't worry about the numbers so much. You're just building an image of this animal in your mind, visualizing it filling its tracks.

The tracks show five toes on each foot. For medium and large mammals, the presence of five toes on the front and

The only families of medium to large animals with five toes front and rear are bear (a), raccoon (b), and weasel (c).

Rabbits have oversized back legs and prefer to hop or bound.

rear feet means that it is in the order Carnivora. In fact, it has to be in the bear, weasel, or raccoon families, since the other North American carnivores have four toes on the front and rear feet. The fact that it's a carnivore actually tells you more about the skull and skeleton of the animal than it does about its eating habits. Most members of this order eat a range of foods, including meat.

Which pair of feet is larger tells you which half of the body carries the most weight. Think of a *Tyrannosaurus rex* and those puny arms. All of a *T. rex*'s weight is on its giant hind feet. Rabbits are a modern example:

Coyotes stand and move up on their toes with their weight forward; they are lean and fast, and their baseline gait is a trot.

small arms, long hind legs, and long, narrow hind feet. Their predominant gait is a bound, which leaves a distinctive track pattern. The size difference between this animal's front and hind tracks is not as great as that between a rabbit's, but it's enough to tell us that black bears are a little back-heavy. Consider the members of the dog family, whose front feet are a bit larger than the hind ones. Their heads and necks extend outward, putting a little more pressure on the front feet than their lean hips put on the hinds. Canine tracks also show only a bit of the foot other than the toes—the small metacarpal, or heel pad. This is common in animals that trot and run a lot, especially those that need to run down rabbits and other prey, such as foxes and coyotes. The bear walks flat-footed, especially on the hind feet, suggesting that it doesn't make a living by running and chasing prey.

Bears are back-heavy and flat-footed and typically move in a walk.

This black bear trail pattern in the dust, which we assume is from the animal's typical gait, looks like the trail of the deer walking in the deep snow, except that the rear tracks don't fall right on top of the front tracks. It is some form of a walk. Given the size of the feet, the spaces between the tracks aren't large enough for this animal to be running. Also, running tracks are less distinct, and some dirt is thrown backward. There is none of that in this trail—it seems like slow, deliberate stepping.

As you can see, there is much more involved than just matching tracks to pictures in a tracking guide. A track is like a miniature representation of the ecology and evolution of the animal that made it. Try to think this way about any sign, no matter how minor. If you trailed this bear, you could discover other clues about its life and identity. The route the trail follows suggests how this animal lives, where it feeds and rests, where it feels safe. Where black bears are hunted, they stick to thick woods and stay away from houses and people. The scat can tell you about its diet and the shifting food resources during the year. You might even find marking trees—signposts for communicating with other bears. These trees often have hairs snagged in the bark, telling you the color and texture of the bear's fur. You could do all this without ever knowing that it was a bear, but you would be seeing what a bear *is*—from the inside out.

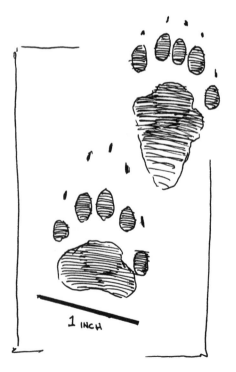

1 INCH

4

Flowers and Trees

There are more plant species around than you will ever get to know, so you need some basis for focusing your search. You can address the most common and abundant species as you encounter them, or you might browse through a local guide to compile a list of common plants. Alternatively, use some other interest of yours to highlight certain species for attention. For example, if you're interested in edible or medicinal plants, use a relevant guide to build a list of species that occur in your range and then pursue their identification. However, if you intend to actually use any of these plants, do yourself a favor and begin by learning which species are toxic and dangerous (try the *Peterson Field Guide to Venomous Animals and Poisonous Plants*). And even then, you have to be very careful about proper identification. When I first got into wild edibles, my enthusiasm to forage outpaced my ability to identify, and I ended up eating the wrong plants by mistake. Fortunately, all I suffered was a stomachache, but it could have been much worse. Don't take any chances.

WILDFLOWERS

Wildflowers are the nonwoody, or herbaceous, plants. This includes what are also known as weeds, those wildflowers that have no idea they are mocking our desire for order and control.

I remember when wildflowers first sprang into my consciousness. I was walking along an old woods road in West Virginia when I noticed a solitary white flower blooming. I was beginning to take an interest in wild things and had been studying trees. I knew many of the common tree names, such as oak, pine, and maple, from my childhood, but I had only recently started to look into what those names meant. In the instant I saw that white bloom in the woods, the term *flower* took on a new meaning. It no longer meant all the cultivated varieties that had blocked my view of the myriad flowering plants that grew according to their own schedules and needs. Once my mind accepted the possibility of wildflowers and all that they implied, my understanding of plants started to change. That little white flower—I have no idea what it was—was the catalyst that changed my whole relationship to the plant world.

The Situation

Imagine that we're walking along a quiet, rural dirt road. This road runs alternately through tunnels of woods and along small lawns and wide open pastures. At one point, the road is bordered on the right by a rocky, wooded slope

On the left are some yellow flowers in a pasture, and on the right are some red flowers under the trees.

and on the left by a pasture. A casual glance into the bright pasture reveals hundreds of small yellow flowers floating above the lengthening grass. Perhaps by chance, or maybe after some close looking, we also notice some fascinating red flowers on the wooded slope.

Taking a Closer Look

Your observations will necessarily be informed by the guide that you're using, but at a minimum, pay attention to flower, branching pattern, and leaf type. A good guide should clearly illustrate and define all the terms used. Most commonly, the front and rear endpapers are filled with illustrations of flower, branch, and leaf forms. These may take a little getting used to, but it's critical that you become familiar with the terms used in your guide. A little attention to this in the beginning will pay off down the road.

The yellow flowers we found are small and numerous on tall, spindly plants. They look like shallow dishes, slightly cupped. Each has five shiny petals. The flower is a *regular* flower, which means that, like a pie, it can be divided along any radius into symmetrical halves. The branching form is *alternate,* meaning that the points where

Tall Buttercup: yellow, regular flowers with five parts; alternate, five-lobed, dissected leaves.

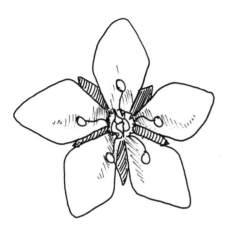

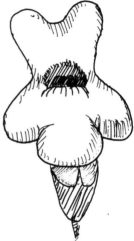

This regular flower can be divided into symmetrical halves along five different axes. An irregular flower has only one axis of symmetry.

the leaves grow from the main stem alternate sides as they go up the stem. The leaves show deep divisions, and all the pointy lobes radiate from a central point, like fingers extending from the palm of a hand. This form may be called palmately lobed, compound, divided, or dissected, depending on your guide. Lobed leaves are like a simple round leaf that has some chunks cut out of it, making baylike areas in the outline. Dissected means the same sort of thing, but with lots of fine cutting. Compound or divided leaves are actually groups of smaller leaflets, serving together as a leaf. In this case, I favor the term dissected or lobed. The terms to use depend on the terms your guide uses. If you are unsure which of two terms in your guide apply to a flower at hand, try each in turn until you get a satisfactory identification.

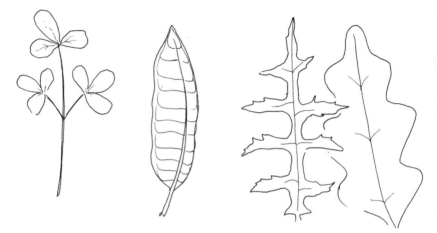

Compound, simple, dissected, and lobed leaves.

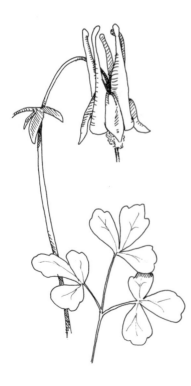

Red Columbine:
red, regular flowers with
alternate, triple-compound
leaves.

Whereas the yellow flower is plain and ordinary, the red flower seems outlandish at first. But on closer inspection, they're not so different. The red flower is regular, with five main parts, and has alternate, palmate leaves. The similarity in form is a clue that these two flowers may be in the same family. This simple outline of traits closely follows family traits, which is why it's helpful to start your closer look there.

Making the Identification

The great thing about most plants is that you can identify them right away based on just a closer look. With these few traits firmly in mind, you can begin to sift through the species presented in your find guide to find the one you are looking at. The Peterson guides, which have regional volumes covering all of North America, are arranged by color. So in the section on yellow flowers, you'll have to search for the illustration of the pasture flower. These guides group species with similar flower and leaf shapes together within their respective colors. Page headings describe the key traits illustrated on the facing page, so you can quickly scan these as you also look for plants that resemble yours.

If you know the family of your flower, you can proceed in one of three ways. If you know that the flower is orchid, for example, you can go to the appropriate color section and flip through it, looking for the icon in the margin that identifies the orchid family. A more efficient way is to go to the introductory chapter and find the family description for orchids, along with page references for that family in each of the sections. Or you could go to the index entry for orchids and find the pages that cover those plants in the appropriate color section.

Those in the Northeast have the advantage of *Newcomb's Wildflower Guide,* which is keyed to the very traits we've been discussing. There is a numerical code that you apply based on flower, branch, and leaf forms. Then you find the page references for that code, where the flower you saw should be illustrated and described. There may be similar guides for other regions, so check with some knowledgeable folks, such as members of a local native plant society, for some field guide tips. Beware of guides that feature close-up photos of just the flower. These photos are beautiful to look at, but they rarely capture the scope of information contained in the drawings in the Peterson or similar guides. Photographs aren't necessarily bad, but the details of flower, branch, and leaf structure are best illustrated by an artist's hand.

Whatever guide you use, the observations you just made should get you to the right part of the book. But you should be prepared to find a number of species on those pages that share the same basic qualities. These are the closely related species, most likely of the same genus as the plant you hope to identify. If this is the case, you'll probably need to draw on a few additional observations to be completely sure of the identification. A species may be distinguished from its relatives by fine hairs on the stem or petals, the relative length and width of leaflets, the way the leaf attaches to the stem, or other details that you are unlikely to consider without the prompting of your guide. Such fine details are rarely captured in photographs.

The yellow pasture flower—with its five petals and its deeply lobed, palmate, alternate leaves—will be found among the yellow buttercups. Once you get to that section of your guide, the height of the plant marks it as the Tall Buttercup (*Ranunculus acris*). Although the Tall Buttercup is rather distinctive, there are other similar yellow *Ranunculus* species. The Bulbous Buttercup, for example, differs in having reflexed sepals under the open flower and swelling at the base of the stem.

Four members of the buttercup family (Ranunculacae). Two are true buttercups. All have regular, five-part flowers and compound or dissected leaves divided by threes or fives. Top left to bottom right: Yellow-flowered Water Buttercup, White Baneberry, Creeping Buttercup, Dwarf Larkspur.

The red flower turns out to be the Red Columbine (*Aquilegia canadensis*). Its five long spurs and divided leaves are unmistakable, resembling only the cultivated variety of columbine. The columbine is so striking and fantastic in appearance that it might be easy to overlook its essential similarities to the Tall Buttercup. As it is, the two plants are of the same family, Ranunculaceae, the Buttercups. Typical members of this family have flowers with five main parts and a bushy button of stamens and pistils in the center; the leaves are divided in groups of either threes or fives.

You'll get to know the families as you identify individual species. Use each new species as an opportunity to figure out its family, and soon you'll be able to place unknown flowers in the right families and identify them. Luckily, plants sit still, so you can go through this process slowly and deliberately with the plant right in front of you. For the most part, if you can reexamine the flower based on questions prompted by the guide, you'll be able to identify it. Concentrating on structural traits and searching in family terms will make the process go more smoothly. These structural, family traits are the signature of how a plant manages pollination and seed dispersal. It is these processes that give the flower "meaning."

The buttercup, for example, has small flattish flower disks. They smell good and are upward-facing, with small bees crawling about inside them. These bees are feeding on nectar and collecting pollen, but as they do so, they carry pollen from one flower to another, fertilizing them and allowing seeds to develop. Every flower needs some way to move pollen from the stamen of one flower to the pistil of another. Since the plants can't move, they must rely on either wind or animals to do the work for them. The structure of a flower is a mix of the original family traits and adaptations to a certain scheme of pollination.

The columbine is a wonder. Its downward-facing flowers look like a bundle of long, red funnels. Each funnel has a long spur that extends backward from the opening and ends in a small bubble. These long, tubular flowers are adapted to

Birds and bees are active pollinators of different kinds of flowers.

specialized nectar-feeding birds and long-tongued insects such as moths. The columbine is clearly animal pollinated. The bubbles at the ends of the spurs store the nectar that the pollinators are searching for. When a hummingbird pokes into a flower for some nectar, it gets pollen on its face. When it visits the next flower, it brings the pollen with it. Transferring pollen from one place to another is incidental to the hummingbird, which is simply trying to feed itself, but the next generation of flowers depends on it.

When a seed germinates at the foot of the parent plant, parent and offspring become competitors for space, light, water, and nutrients. (This might sound familiar to some of you with grown or growing children.) It's in the interest of both to get the seeds away from the parent plant. Almost everyone has had experience with the milkweed, which, like the familiar dandelion, relies on the wind to disperse its seeds. This accounts in part for its ability to colonize almost any patch of open ground. Seeds of other plants have Velcro-like prickles that allow them to cling to fur and be carried to new sites. Fruits with sweet flesh, such as berries, encourage birds and bears and other animals to eat them and disperse the seeds in their droppings. Violets rely on ants to disperse their seeds. Violet seeds have fruitlike nuggets attached to them. The ants eat the fruits and discard the seeds in their underground nests. The seeds sprout from where they were "planted" by the ants.

The physical tools that correspond to the ecological functions of pollination and seed dispersal define the plant families. Each family demonstrates some collection of structural traits and associated behaviors that distinguishes it from other families. With birds, we look at the bill, wing,

*Milkweed seeds are
dispersed by the wind.
The seeds of violets are
dispersed by ants.*

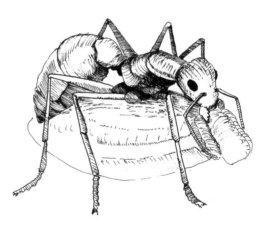

and tail; when tracking mammals, we consider feet and legs. With plants, we look at flower, fruit, leaf, and branch.

The problem with plants is that in any one area, there are more plant families represented by wildflowers than there are bird and mammal families combined. Many people apply only the family name to many plants—such as with milkweed, cattail, grass, reed, mint, and violet—never going any further in identification. My field guides for the northeastern United States list thirty-one and thirty-nine species of violet, respectively. *The Flora of the State of Vermont* lists twenty-seven species in that state alone. One summer, I had a great time learning to identify violets down to the species. Even some of my naturalist friends thought I was crazy (again). For many plants, knowing the family or perhaps a few major groups, or tribes, within the

Top left to bottom right: Representatives of the sunflower tribe of the Compositae family and the violet, lily, and mint families.

family will be enough. For instance, most folks probably know only the most common species of goldenrod, aster, and sunflower, the tribes of the Compositae family. Regardless of how you proceed, you can start by using these core traits to narrow your search.

Ecological factors can be a shortcut to separating species within a family. What are the odds of seeing a Yellow-Flowered Water Buttercup growing out in that pasture? About zero. But look at the illustration a few pages back and notice that it has a typical buttercup flower and five-part, divided leaves. Note the thready leaves, which are similar to those of other water-living plants. You might have guessed that it lives inundated in water just from the illustration in your guidebook.

A good species description should include reference to the habitats or microhabitats where you would expect to find the plant. These big-picture concerns might consist of only a word or two in the text, but they capture 90 percent of your experience of the plant in the field. The most difficult aspect of learning about plants is not identifying them but taking the abundance and profusion of plants you _could_ learn about and putting them together in your head in a meaningful way. Most people fail to remember what they see in the woods because they fail to understand, to contextualize. They overlook the larger story weaving the facts together and bringing them to life.

Taking a Broader Look

Our example is set in the spring. Buttercups and columbines bloom early, and by late summer, their flowers are long gone; only their green parts and maybe the dried fruit bodies remain. These flowers were just two of a host of wildflowers blooming around that time, many of which have completely disappeared. In late summer, goldenrods and then asters dominate the pasture. Only a few flowers can be found on the rocky, shady slope. Those plants flourish (which means "to flower") in the early spring, before the canopy above has matured and robbed them of most of their sunlight. When the flowers are gone, a thick cover of green leaves remains.

As you get to know species and families, you'll be able to identify some plants from the dried structures—dead stalks and fruit pods—that remain visible throughout the nonblooming season. For the most part, though, as you look through your guide to identify a flower, be sure to consider the blooming season as listed in the species accounts. Although the timing of the bloom can vary somewhat, depending on local conditions, the overall range is a handy rule. It can make a real difference in which plant you choose in the end.

As always, the range of the plant is important to consider. Ranges for most of the flowering plants are rather large and are not as clearly delineated as those of mammal species, but range information can still help exclude some closely related species from consideration. Is the site where the plant is growing wet or dry? Is it open and sunny, or a dense thicket? Is the site "disturbed" or a "waste place"? Perhaps the most important big-picture consideration with plants is the character of the site. The most important site qualities are soil nutrients and moisture, openness, and disturbance. These are the essential factors that affect plant survival.

Soil nutrients and moisture are complementary characteristics, since adequate moisture aids in breaking down
leaves and other debris, returning nutrients to the soil. The
underlying geology influences the nutrients available in the
soil, as does the topography. A high, rocky ridge has thin,
poor soil relative to the rich soil of low valleys. Openness,
and therefore access to sunlight, has an obvious effect on
growing conditions. Disturbed sites or waste places include
roadsides, abandoned fields or lots, or riverbanks—anywhere activity has upset the natural vegetation and broken
up the soil.

Some species of wildflowers and trees are able to establish themselves quickly in disturbed sites. Other species take
longer to eventually establish themselves in stable sites,
such as woodlands that have been spared logging for a few
decades. Sites with recent or frequent disturbance favor
quick-growing plants that channel most of their growth into
seed production. These tend to be annual herbs and trees
that rely on wind for pollination and seed dispersal. Had the
site not been disturbed, a different collection of plants
would dominate. In stable woodlands, the wildflowers tend
to be perennials that produce few seeds but grow large
roots, allowing the plant to persist from season to season.
Wind is less reliable for pollination under the forest canopy,
so understory plants there tend to rely on insects or other
animals for pollination and seed dispersal.

In our example, the pasture with the buttercups slopes
gradually down to a low area of mostly shrubs and cattails.
This is a wet, marshy spot where water seeps up from a
spring and flows along the ground to the pond below. The
buttercups are crowded into the lower half of the pasture,

where the soil is obviously moister. The pasture is open, and it is also subject to regular disturbance from rotational grazing and hay cutting. The grazing and cutting make the pasture inhospitable for any trees that might want to sprout there, but there is ample opportunity for the buttercups to grow and thrive between cuts. In contrast, no buttercups can be found growing in the lawns of the nearby farm, where the mowing is finer and more frequent.

The columbine is growing under the canopy of the woods, in a site that is both darker and rockier than the open, moist meadow. I would guess that this site is nutrient poor. It's a stable site, as evidenced by the relatively few flowers the columbine produces compared with the butter-cup, which can have dozens of flowers per plant.

Why worry about the site if you can identify a plant based strictly on its physical appearance? Site conditions can help separate species, such as the Smooth and Downy Wood Violets. Site preferences are also a clue to abundance. If a plant grows in disturbed sites, it's likely to have spread throughout most of the continent. Finally, there are many species that may be mentioned in your guide but not illus-trated due to lack of space. Site conditions are often the best way to recognize these. But the real value of site conditions goes beyond simple plant identification, and is elaborated upon in the next section.

TREES

What is true for wildflowers is also true for trees, with some minor differences. The big difference between trees and most wildflowers is that trees persist throughout the year,

The swampy area below the pasture.

while most plants disappear entirely in winter. The distinction between trees and wildflowers is handy, but it is not a true biological classification. Flower structure figures into the biological classification of plants regardless of whether there is a woody trunk. For example, the rose family includes cherry trees and raspberry bushes, as well as roses. Nevertheless, trees have many distinctive attributes by which we can identify them—things that wildflowers lack.

The Situation
In the same place where we found the buttercups and columbines, there are a number of trees. Among the shrubs and cattails in the swampy area below the pasture, there is a tall, thin tree with needles growing along its branches.

Most people would probably call this a "pine tree" on account of the needles, but is that really what it is?

Taking a Closer Look

When you look at trees, you should focus on the leaves, the branching pattern, and the bark. Notice the similarity between this process and what we did for the wildflowers. You should also note any fruits on or beneath the tree. All these are structural traits analogous to a bird's beak or a mammal's feet. Leaves come in a variety of shapes that should be illustrated and described in your field guide. Some leaves are shaped like needles or overlapping scales, and others are broad and flat. The term *conifer* means "cone-bearing tree" and is generally applied to the needle-leaved trees. These trees tend to have cones as fruit (only pines have "pinecones") and are evergreen. They also tend to have soft wood so are sometimes called softwoods.

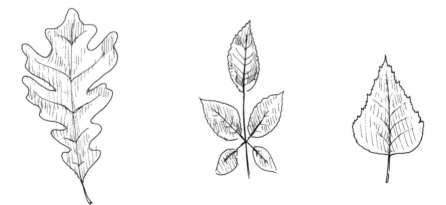

Tree leaves: simple, toothed; palmately compound, toothed; lobed, entire.

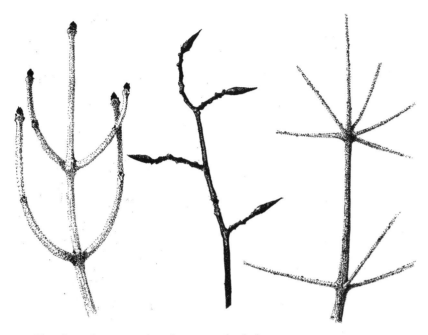

Tree branches: opposite, alternate, whorled.

The branching pattern of trees is similar to that of flowers. Branches can be alternate, they can grow opposite one another, or they can grow in whorls, radiating out from the central stem. Branching pattern is not always noted in species descriptions, but it can be quite helpful. Generally, there is a distinction between the alternate-branched species and the less common opposite-branched trees. Most of the needle-bearing trees are alternate, with a tendency toward whorls.

Along with branching pattern, consider the overall shape of the tree. The growth form of a tree is called its habit. Many guides have pictures of tree habits, but the illustrations assume that the tree grows in the open, with no restrictions on available light. Conifers are more likely than deciduous trees to exhibit the habits illustrated in books. A good illustration of a tree's silhouette and a written description of the tree's overall appearance often capture the essential qualities of branching and shape that you see in the field.

Bark can be very distinctive, but I find it hard to describe in words. *The Audubon Field Guide to Trees* is illustrated with small, close-up photos of bark, which I find very useful. Remember, however, that bark character changes with age, so the bark of a young tree may not look like that of the mature tree pictured in your guide.

The tree we found in the swamp has a thin cone shape with a pointy but sparse canopy. The branches are mostly alternate, nearly whorled, and the bark is gray and flaky. The most important observation is that the tree has needles. If you consulted your field guide at this point, looking for needles, you would find that you need more information. How are the needles arranged on the branch? Are the needles in bundles or clusters? Are there more than five needles in a bundle or cluster? You will see that most of the needle-bearing trees in North America fall into one family, Pinaceae, the pines. Within this large family are a few distinct genera, each with numerous species that are good units for narrowing the search: spruce, pine, fir, hemlock, and a few others. These species can be told apart on the basis of needle arrangement alone: Pine needles grow in groups of two to five bundled needles, with the base of the bundle wrapped in a papery sheath. Spruce needles grow singly and are sharply pointed and four-angled. Only the

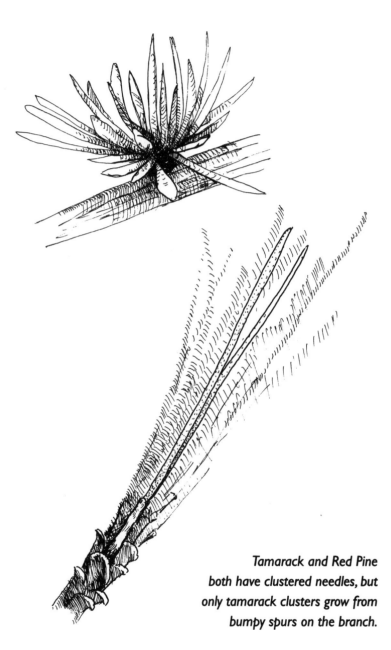

*Tamarack and Red Pine
both have clustered needles, but
only tamarack clusters grow from
bumpy spurs on the branch.*

larches have more than five needles in each unsheathed cluster growing from bumpy "spurs" on the branches. The needles on your tree arise in a circular, fanlike cluster. Looking at the whole tree up close, you can see these sprays of needles along every branch. The needles themselves are about an inch long. The cones are small, not even an inch long, with a few thin, flexible scales.

Making the Identification

This is enough information to make the identification. For tree and shrub identification, I mainly use two guides in tandem. The first, *The National Audubon Society Field Guide to North American Trees,* is illustrated with photographs and arranged by leaf shape. You go to the appropriate section of photo plates and search for a matching leaf. Along with the leaf photo is a photo of the bark for comparison. There are also sections for fruits, flowers, and even autumn foliage colors of selected species. Once the appropriate picture is found, you are referred to the species description in the back of the book. The second guide, *Trees and Shrubs,* is the Peterson guide for trees of the East. It has no photographs but uses a keying system to walk you through some simple descriptions. As you answer yes or no to each successive question, you narrow down the list of possibilities. At some point, you will be sent to a listing of particular species, and you can pick yours out of the lineup. The illustrations are leaf- and branch-based schematic drawings supplemented by written species accounts. The resulting arrangement puts similar species side by side, with notes on the particular differences between them.

The Peterson and Audubon guides both demonstrate a trend to try to make things easier on the user by minimizing the need to learn new terminology or read through written descriptions. My general opinion is that this just makes things harder in the long run. Often the information that a beginner really needs to learn is cut out of the guide. In this case, however, I think the keys in the Peterson guide are accessible and helpful, and the format of the Audubon guide works well and doesn't hinder the ability to learn more about how to identify trees as you go. The two complement each other nicely.

Based on your closer look, the field has been narrowed to the European and American Larches, but which is which? The species descriptions reveal that the bark and the branchlets are different and that the European Larch has longer needles and cones, but these differences aren't the important ones. The primary difference has nothing to do with how the tree looks but rather where it is found.

The European Larch is an introduced tree. I wouldn't expect to find it far from human habitation, and this site is right on a farm. This spot has been continuously inhabited by people of European descent for over 200 years. Could one of them have planted a European Larch here? Maybe, but the site is also very wet. Most descriptions of the American Larch mention swampy or boggy soils, whereas the European Larch is said to be more of an upland species. A tree's site preference really refers to the conditions necessary for its seeds to germinate. Trees can be transplanted to sites outside of those "preferred" conditions, but why bring a tree all the way from another continent just to plant it in a

*Key features of Tamarack:
tree growth form, leaves
(needles), and fruit (cones).*

cold, wet bog? So I think we're justified in concluding that it's an American Larch, or, as folks around here call it, Tamarack.

The Tamarack site contains plenty of short, broad-leaved shrubs as well. (Broad-leaved trees are also called

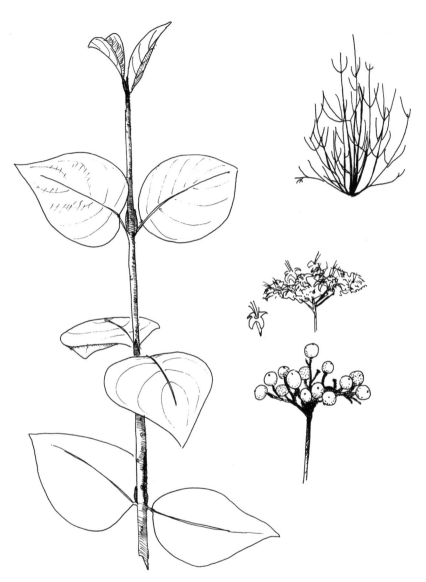

Red-osier Dogwood: opposite, simple, entire leaves and bright red bark. In spring, there are four-part flowers; in fall, white berries. Notice the interesting pattern of the veins on the leaves.

hardwoods.) The leaves are simple, lack toothed margins, and are oval shaped. The leaves are opposite one another on the stems, and they have an interesting pattern of venation. The prominent veins that branch outward from the center of the leaf sweep in an arc toward the leaf tip. The stems are numerous and small, so the bark is not thick and rough but more like a smooth skin. In this case, it is also bright red. In the spring, you might see flat-topped clusters of four-petaled flowers. Later in summer and into the fall, these flowers turn into clusters of white berries.

It's not hard to get to the right place in your field guide based on the opposite, simple leaves, but ultimately, the red stems are the real give-away that this is Red-osier Dogwood. The species description should also mention that this shrub is common in wetlands. The four-part flowers and the flower clusters are typical of the dogwood family, as is the venation of the leaves. This is an example of the myriad finer details that you will explore as you identify species, but remember that the main structural components, such as branching pattern and flower shape, are what these finer observations are based on.

The Peterson field guides and some other specialty, regional guides have keys for twigs and buds in addition to leaves. The winter buds, which will be next spring's leaves, can be more distinctive than the leaves themselves, as in the case of Red and Sugar Maples. I think that people who learn their trees in the winter learn them better. Maybe they are forced to take a closer look without the leaves to rely on. And when spring comes, it's a singular pleasure to watch the new leaves unfold.

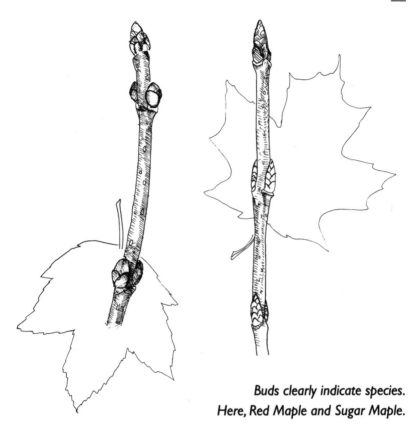

Buds clearly indicate species.
Here, Red Maple and Sugar Maple.

Taking a Broader Look

Species descriptions often include reference to site conditions such as soil, moisture, and sunlight. Soil is the source of nutrients for plants, and wetter sites tend to have richer soils, especially if there are lots of leaves and other organic debris. If the soil is too wet and cold, however, the organic matter can't break down, so the site will be nutrient poor. Areas with closed canopies tend to be wetter and colder

Southern exposures (a) can mean warmer, drier conditions than on the north slope (c). Elevation and wind can also dry out high sites (b). High sites tend to have less soil of poorer quality than valley sites (d), where soil and moisture accumulate.

than those that are open. The topography can have an influence as well. Ridges often have thin soil and might be subject to drying winds, whereas valley bottoms usually have richer soil due to flooding and runoff from the surrounding hills. South-facing slopes are more likely to have species that prefer warmer and drier conditions than are north-facing slopes.

Knowing the site preferences of common species will help you identify the trees and other plants you come across. Balsam Fir and Eastern Hemlock are common in these woods. Hemlocks are found in moist, well-drained woods, and firs are most likely to be found in moist woods and bottomlands. Both could be found in the area where we were tracking the deer in chapter 3—a dark, moist place where conifers tend to do better than in warmer sites. Sugar maples and other species that thrive in all conditions would also be found there, but dry-site or open-country species would be absent. Fir and hemlock are superficially similar in appearance, and both have flat needles. Because they are so similar, the field guide descriptions highlight their differences. By absorbing this information ahead of time, you can spend your time in the field getting to know these trees and building your personal experience with each species. Pay attention to how each plant fits into the wider landscape, and you will understand them in relation to a dynamic, living ecological community.

A plant community is a collection of trees and other plants that thrives under similar conditions of soil, moisture, and sunlight. We usually name communities by the trees that dominate them. The plant community defines the habitat and forms the basis of the animal community that inhabits the area. Some specialist plants grow only under a narrow range of conditions and are clear indicators of site conditions. Tamarack is one of these. Tamarack thrives in boggy, wet sites. Bogs are places where cold temperatures and stagnant water lead to acidic and oxygen-poor conditions that only certain kinds of plants and animals can tolerate. As you look around a little more, you will notice a marked difference between the plants in this small wetland and the surrounding forests and fields. The species of trees supported in the wetland are almost completely absent from the woods nearby. You could walk around all day and not find a single Tamarack in the surrounding hills. The hillsides around the wetlands support a different community of trees and shrubs.

Along with wetland specialists such as the Tamarack and Red-osier Dogwood, this site supports a few Big-toothed Aspen and Sugar Maple saplings. The aspen is an opportunist that is quick to sprout wherever there is abundant sunshine. The Sugar Maple is a generalist—a jack-of-all-trades in Vermont—and is likely to sprout almost anywhere. It can handle the full sun of this site as well as the shade of a mature forest canopy.

As you learn about plants, you're discovering not only their associations with one another and with the particular site but also their associations with animals that you may be tracking. In this swamp, both Tamarack and the understory of Red-osier Dogwood provide food for songbirds and other animals. The whole site is also covered with cattails, which provide seeds for songbirds and small mammals and nesting cover for many others, particularly Red-winged Blackbirds, Mallards, and Black Ducks. Snowshoe hare browse the dogwood, voles and lemmings tunnel through the low growth, and all are hunted by weasels, fishers, and red foxes.

Not far from this spot are steep, rocky ledges. They face south, making them a little warmer than the Tamarack site. Oaks, absent from the wetland, thrive at these ledges. Porcupines and bobcats are common there, as both use the ledges for protection. Bobcats like the warm exposure, and porcupines take advantage of the ledges and caves for dens and feed on the acorns.

With a little experience, you will soon find yourself in an interesting position. When you find a new plant, you may know that you've never seen it before, but you may have a strong suspicion about what it might be. This is my goal whenever I go into the field. This ability comes from having good observation skills and a decent number of species and families filed away in your brain. So when you encounter some new, unknown plant, you are able to understand something about it based on where it is and what it looks like. It becomes linked to similar plants you've already identified and the images you've seen while flipping through your field guides. The result is a strong feeling about what it could be. You could never have imagined this happening back when plants were just a confusing "wall of green." But this is what happens when you understand the ecology behind the appearance of things. By using the methods described in this book, you will reach this place much sooner than if you were working only with a field guide and no sense of the bigger picture.

5

A Natural History
Mystery

Here is a simple tracking mystery that exposed some of the most profound patterns in nature to me. This experience taught me that the tracks we find are not simply signs of an animal or a single event, but rather snapshots of a dynamic relationship connecting plants and animals to a place through the long reach of time. It illustrates the methods of this book as well as the nature of ecological communities.

I used to spend a lot of time wandering among the mesquite-saguaro-paloverde scrublands in southern Arizona. One day, below a street sign right where the pavement ended and the sand began, I found a pile of small seeds clumped together in a reddish mass. This odd sign captivated me. I can still remember the texture and color of the seeds and the sticky red jelly that covered them. From my prior foraging and exploring, I knew that they were not from mesquite or any of the other common trees, grasses, or cacti. It was really quite beautiful, but I had no idea what plant these seeds had come from or how they had gotten there. I spent some time just looking at the seeds, trying to see them as thoroughly as I could so that I would recognize them again if I had the chance. They were football shaped and a few millimeters long. Each seed had a few black stripes running the long way. The overall color looked yellowish or tan, but the seeds were embedded in a thin, very sticky, pinkish goo.

Once I got an eyeful of the close-up view, I started moving my perspective outward. I examined the ground all around the pile looking for any marks that might indicate an animal walking up and leaving the seeds there. I didn't recognize anything on the ground, so I let my eyes and mind continue to spread out around the whole scene. I found that there were other seeds clinging to the signpost and a small clump on top of it. Confirming my growing suspicion that the seeds were some kind of bird droppings were white streaks in some of the seed piles and some bird whitewash on the sand. Again, there were no tracks that I could discern, which allowed me to rule out many of the common ground-foraging birds in the area, such as Gambel's Quail. It was a big pile containing at least a cup of seeds, and there was no sign that the bird was feeding on anything but the single fruit that carried this seed.

Since it was bird sign, there was no trail to follow—or was there? Awakened to this clump-of-seeds phenomenon, I soon found several similar sites, including a roost I had noticed in the past. Without investigating it closely, I had passed it off as a fungus attacking a twig. All the seed piles were composed of a large amount of only this one particular seed. The amount of seeds and the conditions of the roost suggested repetitive events—there were just too many seeds on small roost twigs for it to be anything but a smallish bird coming back over and over again. Each was on the highest point of whatever object it adorned—generally shrubs and low trees—with some spillage on the ground. At this point, I wasn't building a list and eliminating possibilities. Rather, I was letting observations and inferences accumulate and sit in the back of my mind. I was subtly building a portrait of the roosts, trusting that in time it would lead me to a bird. The high roosts meant that the bird was probably conspicuous, and I was starting to think that the complete adherence to this one kind of fruit had to be noted in some of the references.

In a sense, I wasn't tracking a bird or a plant. I was tracking both, or, more accurately, the relationship between them. But I couldn't put it all together until I knew enough to identify one of the players. I could have staked out a roost and waited for it to be used. I could have noticed which birds frequented the area and paid particular attention to those that roosted atop shrubs. Then, among the birds that fit the bill, I could have searched for the ones that subsisted on fruit, specifically, one particular type of fruit. Had I done that, I might have begun to unravel a great story. As it worked out, the revelation came when I was pursuing other questions, particularly about mesquite trees.

Mesquite trees were largely confined to the washes and riparian areas of the arid Southwest when the Europeans arrived. Periodic floods scarified the thick coats of the mesquite seeds, allowing them to germinate. In more recent times, mesquite began poking up in the grasslands and flats where newly introduced cattle were grazing. Some trees were cut for lumber and firewood, but many of them were simply torn up to keep the rangelands clear—with only mixed success. New trees kept sprouting up among the cows. The most effective way to clear away mesquite is to drain underground aquifers, leaving an area too dry for even the long roots of mesquite to survive.

It turns out that the cows themselves were bringing the mesquite out of the washes and into the rangelands. The long beanlike mesquite pods are sweet, and the cows were eating them. The tough seeds would then pass through their digestive systems intact and fall, with ample fertilizer, around the range. These sweet pods with their hard seeds had evolved through the relationship between the mesquite trees and some now-extinct herbivores. Those browsers and grazers ate the pods and dispersed the seeds, but the seeds had to be tough to withstand the journey. Once the Pleistocene herbivores disappeared, only raging floodwaters could wake up the true viability of the seeds. After the cows arrived, however, there was a new agent to disperse the seeds throughout their grassy ranges, just as the giant ground sloths once did.

As I was studying mesquite trees, trying to get to know the whole cactus-scrub community, I happened to uncover the relationship among them; the desert mistletoe, which is a parasite of mesquites; and the Phainopepla, a bird that is the primary disperser of desert mistletoe berries. Reading about this link reminded me of something a friend in the Forest Service had told me years before. She had been trying to control the spread of mistletoe in the foothills of southern California and described how the seeds were encased in a goo that made them stick to tree branches, where they could germinate and tap into the new host.

That was my "Aha!" moment. My mind flashed to images of hundreds of local sightings of male and female Phainopeplas cutting through the air currents between their high roosts. The Phainopepla, it turns out, has a gut that is specially adapted for removing the flesh from mistletoe berries and then leaving the sticky seeds as droppings. Phainopeplas carry the mistletoe seeds from tree to tree, where the seeds stick and then sprout into uninfected mesquite trees. Over the following weeks, this new information led my quest to verify that the seed piles were indeed the roosts of Phainopeplas and that the seeds were the residue of their feeding on desert mistletoe.

Solving this riddle had as much to do with the information I read at home as with the observations I made in the field. I wasn't even trying to solve the mystery when the answer became clear. I was carrying that mystery in the back of my mind, along with many others. It was the web of ecological relationships among all the different pieces that allowed my field time and my book time to complement each other perfectly.

Having come to the answer the long way around, I had a greater understanding of the life of the area and the crucial ecological relationships that play out when I'm not looking. Instead of just seeing Phainopeplas flying through the air, I could "see" them feeding on and coevolving with desert mistletoe, participating in a dynamic landscape of trees and animals ebbing, flowing, and changing through time.

This is my favorite kind of tracking experience—one where understanding the sign demands an awareness of both the plants and the animals around you. Every piece of the story contains dynamic links extending across the land and through time. As always, there is more to the story; some is known, but much is unknown. The answer to each riddle is just the introduction to the next.

6

Field Guides
and Other Resources

There are a lot of references available, but they are not all equally suited to our purposes. To get started as a naturalist, you need good field guides for the details of identification, natural histories to build the big picture in terms of species and families, and everything else to stoke the fires of curiosity.

I think it's a good policy to have at least two field guides for the subjects that really interest you. Choose the primary guide to tell you what to look for to identify a subject. Choose the second for an extra illustration and a little more depth in subspecies information or natural history. I have four tracking guides, three tree guides plus another one dedicated to shrubs, three bird guides, and two for wildflowers. These are the field guides that I actively use. In addition, have behavior or natural history guides to complement the field guides. These books cover background and descriptive information that isn't necessarily intended to be used for identification purposes.

I used to be convinced that paintings were better than photos in field guides, but I'm beginning to waver. Modern photo editing has come a long way, but still, photos usually don't show natural or baseline postures. This can complicate the kind of subconscious comparison and image building you do as you flip through the guide. I tend to prefer good baseline postures to "nonstandard" postures in a primary identification guide. You want to see the subject's "average" appearance and diagnostic features, and paintings and drawings can often do a better job of representing these. Whatever the method of illustration, compare your guide with others to make sure you're getting the fullest picture of the subject possible.

Illustrations are critical, but they should be backed up with good text. A good guide should show you each species and its range. It should describe differences in appearance based on sex, age, or geography, and illustrate them when necessary. It should accentuate specific differences but also convey the common characteristics of appearance, behavior, and habitat by phylogenetic groupings. The ideal situation is to have all the information pertaining to a given species together. A little natural history information, such as habitat, food habits, courtship, and reproductive periods, is nice but not essential.

Lots of guides try to cover everything from wildflowers to birds to fish. I'm not a fan of these. They generally offer only a selection of species from each group, and they are often weak at key features of identification. These are the guides that show close-up photos of wildflowers but nothing of the leaves or other features. Beware of too little information. Other guides are advertised as "local" guides (I'm not talking about regional versions of Sibley's or Peterson's) or beginner's guides. These guides have the appeal of being small and simple in presentation, so the topic seems accessible to beginners. However, I'm wary of any guide that offers "less" as a selling point. Unfortunately, loss of quality often accompanies the simplification process. Good beginner's books are those that give some background information and pointers to help you use your primary guide. These books may be worthwhile if you want something small to carry into the field to jog your memory, but if you are serious about exploring the subject, invest in a full-fledged field guide.

My minimum book list for the topics covered in this book is as follows:

1. *Ecology of Eastern/Western Forests* (Peterson)
2. *National Geographic Field Guide to Birds of North America*
3. *Lives of North American Birds*
4. *Mammal Tracks and Sign* (Elbroch) or *Tracking and the Art of Seeing* (Rezendes)
5. *Kaufman In-Focus Mammals*
6. *Trees and Shrubs/Western Trees* (Peterson)
7. *Newcomb's Wildflower Guide* or Peterson's regional wildflower guides

The following sections describe these and other guides in more detail.

ECOLOGY

Primary Guide

Ecology of Eastern/Western Forests, Peterson Field Guides (John C. Kricher and Gordon Morrison).

This is the best book to get you started. It isn't an identification guide or even a field guide per se; rather, it is a map to the ecological communities in which you live. In addition to community descriptions and species lists, it is full of interesting essays on key ecological patterns that provide background to your experiences in the woods.

Natural History

Reading the Forested Landscape (Tom Wessels).

This is the definitive book on interpreting the natural and cultural history of a site by examining what is growing there and how it is growing. Although it is grounded in the study of the ecological communities of central New England, the principles are applicable everywhere.

The Trees in My Forest (Bernd Heinrich).

A naturalist's look at the trees of the northern hardwood-boreal forests of Maine. This entertaining book highlights the biology of trees and the ecology of their interactions within the larger forest community.

The North Woods (Peter J. Marchand).

A readable treatment of the dynamic ecological community of the boreal forest of North America. It establishes a basic understanding of the forces of nature and time that go into shaping a plant community.

Life in the Cold (Peter J. Marchand).

A readable text of interest to anyone exposed to winter climes. It conveys an understanding of ecology that can be readily applied to other environments as well.

Science

Ecology: Concepts and Applications (Manuel C. Molles Jr.) and *Concepts of Ecology* (Edward J. Kormondy).

Both books are used as introductory texts for ecology courses. The Kormondy book is more accessible to the lay reader.

BIRDS

These five things are important in bird guides:
1. All species information (picture, range map, species account) located together.
2. Multiple species per page for direct comparison.
3. Information on similar species and how to tell them apart.
4. Organized phylogenetically with descriptions of families.
5. Field marks indicated in text and on illustrations.

Primary Guides

National Geographic Field Guide to the Birds of North America
- <u>Best points</u>: All of North America in a small package; nice, lively illustrations; all species information grouped together; phylogenetic order.
- <u>Weak points</u>: Scant natural history information.

- <u>Bottom line</u>: My recommendation as the best identification guide.

Peterson Field Guide to Eastern/Western Birds
- <u>Best points</u>: Good baseline paintings with field mark indicators (arrows in pictures, italics in text); similar species descriptions in text; silhouettes on inside covers; phylogenetic order.
- <u>Weak points</u>: Range maps located in appendix separate from illustrations and text.
- <u>Bottom line</u>: The classic, gold-standard, field guide; excellent except for the maps.

Kaufman Field Guide to Birds of North America
- <u>Best points</u>: Clearly indicated field marks and clear descriptions for identification; great "how to use this book" system.
- <u>Weak points</u>: Very "busy" presentation (up to fifteen birds per plate).
- <u>Bottom line</u>: A good identification guide.

Sibley Field Guide to Birds of Eastern/Western North America
- <u>Best points</u>: Beautiful paintings; detailed information on and presentation of age, sex, and subspecies appearances.
- <u>Weak points</u>: Lacks more general information.
- <u>Bottom line</u>: Great guide for more experienced birders.

Smithsonian Handbooks Birds of North America (and smaller regional volumes)

- <u>Best points</u>: A wealth of information on identification and natural history, including flight patterns, nests, and similar species.
- <u>Weak points</u>: Single species per page and nonbaseline poses.
- <u>Bottom line</u>: A great second guide. Maybe one notch better than Stokes (below) as a primary guide.

Stokes Field Guide to Birds Eastern/Western Region

- <u>Best points</u>: Wealth of natural history information; excellent "Learning Pages" and "Guide to Common Birds" sections, giving tips on identification.
- <u>Weak points</u>: Nonstandard poses and families lumped together.
- <u>Bottom line</u>: A great second guide.

National Audubon Society Field Guide to North American Birds (Eastern/Western Region)

- <u>Best points</u>: Nice species accounts.
- <u>Weak points</u>: Photos of nonstandard poses; illustrations are arranged by color and shape of bird, with species accounts in a separate section.
- <u>Bottom line</u>: Not recommended as a primary guide.

"Golden Guide" Birds of North America

- <u>Best points</u>: Baseline paintings, sonograms.
- <u>Weak points</u>: Not as good (less information, less up-to-date) as others currently available.
- <u>Bottom line</u>: Great for children; my son has one.

Natural History

These general references give you depth beyond more picture matching. This information may be immediately practical in terms of identification or useful as background information.

Lives of North American Birds (Kenn Kaufman).

This is the best natural history guide for help in identifying birds. It offers great immediately practical natural history information, along with photographs that often show the birds in poses different from those in field guides. It also includes information on families. This volume is handy for birders, providing some but not too much extra information.

Sibley Guide to Bird Life and Behavior (David Allen Sibley).

This is an incredibly thorough book that explores bird ecology and behavior at the family level. I love it, but it isn't for everyone. Hard-core birders, such as my life-listing, hotline-calling brother, will like it.

The Birder's Handbook (Paul R. Ehrlich, David S. Dobkin, and Darryl Wheye).

This book contains tons of information in the species accounts, but it's not very specific. The best feature is that half the book is dedicated to short essays on all manner of ornithological topics, providing a great backdrop to your growing knowledge of individual species and their families.

Stokes Nature Guides: Guide to Bird Behavior (Donald and Lillian Stokes).

These three volumes offer fantastic accounts of behaviors peculiar to the featured species. They don't give basic natural history information, such as preferred foods, but they tell the life history of the bird and feature behavioral displays that can be observed in the field. These books aren't useful as an adjunct to the identification process, but they add to your understanding of a bird that you've already seen or expect to see.

Beginner's Books

Don't bother with the little books that are just watered-down field guides for beginners. However, the following two books may be useful.

Pete Dunne on Birdwatching (Pete Dunne).

My favorite all-around guide to the activity of bird-watching.

Birding Basics (David Allen Sibley).

A great introduction to birding, with a major emphasis on plumage and appearance.

MAMMALS AND TRACKING

Mammal Field Guides

This is where your success as a tracker begins. Fortunately, the options are few and good. I have always used the *Peterson's Field Guide to Mammals*, despite its shortcomings. In general, you need some information on orders and families, as well as species, and a sense of the size and shape of the animals. A little natural history is nice too.

Kaufman Focus Guide to Mammals of North America and *Princeton Field Guides to Mammals of North America*
- <u>Best points</u>: Both guides are accurate and up-to-date, have good keying systems, and are packed with information.
- <u>Weak points</u>: Phylogeny is lost a little to the keying system—a minor point.
- <u>Bottom line</u>: Both are great field guides, so choose one based on its personal appeal.

National Audubon Society Field Guide to North American Mammals
- <u>Best points</u>: Good species accounts.
- <u>Weak points</u>: Photos separate from text; poor track illustrations.
- <u>Bottom line</u>: A decent secondary reference.

Peterson Field Guide to Mammals: North America North of Mexico
- <u>Best points</u>: Phylogenetic order.
- <u>Weak points</u>: Outdated.
- <u>Bottom line</u>: An updated edition is due soon which will improve this guide's appeal.

Tracking Field Guides

Be sure that your guide includes tracks *and* sign. Many guides try to simplify their presentation by covering only clear tracks. Smaller, local guides provide good information, but if you're buying a guide, I recommend one that can serve as a thorough reference. For this reason, I like the Elbroch book, although it might scare a beginner. The best-case scenario is to have both the Elbroch and the Rezendes books.

Mammal Tracks and Sign (Mark Elbroch)
- <u>Best points</u>: Most thorough guide available; excellent tips on technique, gait information, and other background; more information on smaller mammals than any other tracking guide.
- <u>Weak points</u>: Might be too much for beginners; perhaps best for someone with some exposure to tracking.
- <u>Bottom line</u>: The best reference available on the subject; no serious tracker should be without it.

Tracking and the Art of Seeing (Paul Rezendes)
- <u>Best points</u>: Accessible and thorough treatment of selected species, especially tracks and gaits; photos of feet.
- <u>Weak points</u>: Contains less information and covers fewer species than the Elbroch guide.
- <u>Bottom line</u>: Perhaps the best guide for someone new to tracking.

Mammal Tracking in North America (James Halfpenny).
   A good overview of tracking and the mammals of North America, though a bit technical in tone.

Tracking Animals in Snow (Louise Forrest).

A handy reference covering some of the distortions caused by snow that don't make it into other tracking guides.

Natural History

Stokes Guide to Animal Tracking and Behavior (Donald and Lillian Stokes).

This book stresses that tracking is based on understanding animals. It covers common North American mammals and gives brief synopses of their natural history, along with comments on types of sign.

Background

Mammal (Smithsonian Institution).

This is a beautiful picture book with shots of selected mammals from all over the world. There are short essays on ecological patterns and processes, as well as species descriptions. It's arranged in phylogenetic order, so you can really see what those categories mean in terms of the animals' form and appearance. This book is tailor-made to program your brain to understand mammals. It's a modern incarnation of the *World Book of Mammals* (Crown Press) that my parents gave me when I was eight years old. That book is still on my shelf. I credit the long hours I spent daydreaming over it with my awakening interest in becoming a naturalist.

Animal (Smithsonian Institution).

This is essentially the same as the preceding book but includes birds, reptiles, fish, and so on in addition to mammals.

Life of Mammals (David Attenborough).

A book and a documentary film series. Both illustrate the ecology of mammals by looking in on how they thrive and survive.

TREES

Field Guides

National Audubon Society Field Guide to North American Trees (Eastern/Western Region)
- Best points: Easy to use; includes bark photos and rich species information.
- Weak points: Visual leaf key can be misleading.
- Bottom line: A great guide, but not perfect.

Peterson Field Guide to Trees and Shrubs/Western Trees
- Best points: Easy-to-use botanical keying system.
- Weak points: Not as nice to look at as the Audubon guide.
- Bottom line: A great guide.

The Tree Identification Book and *The Shrub Identification Book* (George W. D. Symonds)
- Best points: Easy to use; thorough visual keys.
- Weak points: A little dated in appearance.
- Bottom line: Great guides, especially the one for shrubs, which usually get short shrift.

Natural History

The Book of Field and Roadside, The Book of Forest and Thicket, and *The Book of Swamp and Bog* (John Eastman and Amelia Hansen).

These books provide incredibly detailed accounts of common plants of the named habitats, with a particular emphasis on ecological interactions, particularly with insects.

Illustrated Book of Trees (William Carey Grimm and John Kartesz).

An old-fashioned botanical guide that uses words you have never heard of before. The down side of that is that it takes some work to learn the vocabulary to use it quickly, but in the end you can be more accurate and exact in your identifications and also learn some old-school botany. Old-school botany has its value to some.

WILDFLOWERS

Field Guides

Peterson Field Guide to Wildflowers: Northeastern and North-Central North America
- <u>Best points</u>: Good drawings, family descriptions, and family "index."
- <u>Weak points</u>: Poor keying.
- <u>Bottom line</u>: The go-to guide.

Newcomb's Wildflower Guide (Lawrence Newcomb)
- <u>Best points</u>: Simple but excellent structural keying system.

- <u>Weak points</u>: Limited to the Northeast.
- <u>Bottom line</u>: My favorite guide for the region it covers. The key is worth a look by those in other regions.

National Audubon Society Field Guide to North American Wildflowers

- <u>Best points</u>: Features good close-up views of flowers and family descriptions.
- <u>Weak points</u>: Emphasis on flower matching de-emphasizes other plant characteristics.
- <u>Bottom line</u>: A decent secondary guide.

Natural History

Illustrated Book of Wildflowers and Shrubs (William Carey Grimm and John T. Kartesz).

See similar listings for trees.

Edible and Medicinal Plants

Use a real field guide to identify such plants, and use these resources for their unique information.

Peterson Field Guide to Venomous Animals and Poisonous Plants.

One-stop shop for the things that could hurt you. A great place to start learning.

Field Guide to Edible Wild Plants and *Field Guide to Medicinal Wild Plants* (Bradford Angier).

Excellent resources from a trusted name on the subject.

Peterson Field Guide to Edible Plants: Eastern and Central North America (Lee Allen Peterson) and *Peterson Field Guide to Medicinal Plants and Herbs: Eastern and Central North America* (Steven Foster and James A. Duke).

Good, thorough guides, including information on which season to collect the plants. I use these as almost encyclopedic references.

Medicinal Plants of the Desert and Canyon West, Medicinal Plants of the Pacific West, and *Medicinal Plants of the Mountain West* (Michael Moore).

These are serious books on medicinal plants and their uses by a professional practitioner. Maybe the best guides on the collection, preparation, and use of wild medicinals.

Index